Effective Communication for Science and Technology

D1322726

Palgrave Study Guides

www.palgravestudyguides.com

Effective Communication for Science and Technology

Joan van Emden

palgrave

First published 2001 by
PALGRAVE
Houndmills, Basingstoke, Hampshire RG21 6XS and
175 Fifth Avenue, New York, N.Y. 10010
Companies and representatives throughout the world

PALGRAVE is the new global academic imprint of
St. Martin's Press LLC Scholarly and Reference Division and
Palgrave Publishers Ltd (formerly Macmillan Press Ltd).

ISBN 0–333–77546–5 paperback

This book is printed on paper suitable for recycling and
made from fully managed and sustained forest sources.

A catalogue record for this book is available
from the British Library.

10 9 8 7 6 5 4 3 2 1
10 09 08 07 06 05 04 03 02 01

Printed in Malaysia

Contents

Preface

Increasingly, communication skills are included in scientific and technical courses at universities and colleges, not as an optional extra but as an integral and important part of a student's work. Employers ask not just for subject qualifications but also for practical skills such as the ability to convey complex information clearly and concisely both in speech and writing.

This book guides students through the main forms of communication which they will need in order to follow their courses successfully and to get jobs at the end. Important tasks included are: reading efficiently and taking notes from lectures, books and the Internet – often overlooked or taken for granted by lecturers and tutors; writing reports and dissertations in an appropriate format and style; making presentations, individually and in groups; preparing thoroughly for a viva, project colloquium or computer demonstration; completing effective application forms and CVs, and succeeding at job interviews.

Each stage is discussed in a friendly and informal way, with examples from a range of scientific and technical subjects. I am very grateful to all my students over many years, who have, either deliberately or by accident, given me useful material to illustrate good and bad practice in writing and in presentations.

In particular, I should like to thank Jennifer Easteal at Salisbury College for her invaluable advice and support; Averil Macdonald and Gavin Maple of the Department of Physics, Chris Stain of the Department of Botany, the Careers Advisory Service, all at the University of Reading, and other departments at the University which sent me useful material; Mark Nelson of Reading Bluecoat School.

I am, as always, indebted to my colleagues Elizabeth Barber, Lucinda Becker and Anne Pinnock for their invaluable help and advice whenever I have needed it, and for the support they have given me. Any mistakes that remain are my own.

Joan van Emden
Reading, 2000

Part One
Introduction

1 At the Beginning of Your Course

The transition from school to further or higher education is often exhilarating and frequently intimidating. The relationship between teacher and taught is different; students no longer have a tightly structured day which they are more or less compelled to follow; the amount of work achieved is largely the concern of the individual; new students suddenly find that they have responsibilities that they have never had to consider before, such as accommodation, food and budgeting. In addition to all these new experiences, they have to face lectures, libraries and other large and initially strange sources of information which they have to access with little guidance, and work is expected of them in forms of which they may have little experience: notes, reports and presentations.

Help is usually given to new students, of course, by lecturers, tutors, library staff and others, who are very aware of the stress that so many new experiences can generate, but the amount of individual help varies between colleges, universities, faculties and departments; it may also depend on the student knowing what and whom to ask. Many of the problems which the new student faces are beyond the scope of this book, but others, involving aspects of communication, are sometimes overlooked: reading and selecting information efficiently, making notes, and using an appropriate format – report or presentation – in a way which is already seen to be professional, and which will provide useful experience for work in the future. Even in the first year of a course, this should be an important consideration for students, as their ability to communicate their scientific or technical expertise may in the long term be almost as important as the facts they are learning.

The aspects of communication which are discussed in this book involve skills which need to be learnt and practised, in conditions which make such study both congenial and challenging. Students have some responsibility for the conditions in which they work, which is why, first of all, I look at ways in which new students can help themselves to study successfully.

▶ Studying effectively

This book will give you help with producing and organising information; it will be invaluable as you start to prepare your assignments, and throughout your course. But before you begin such preparation, it is worth looking briefly at the physical conditions in which you will be studying, and thinking how you can make them comfortable and at the same time conducive to concentrated effort. Where and how can you study most effectively?

You will be spending a great deal of your time receiving information, and this activity will take place initially in lecture rooms or lecture theatres; we will discuss the tasks of listening and taking notes in a later chapter. Where will you carry out your own work? In order to gather material, you may need a library, either the main university or college library or a smaller – and probably less intimidating – library in your faculty or department. Visit the libraries which you are most likely to need, early in your course; try to locate one or two books or journals which you already know about from school or a first lecture, just so that you begin to find your way around; ask a member of the library staff for help if you need it.

You may be fortunate enough to have a guided tour of library facilities; this is a good opportunity to make yourself familiar with the resources you will need, but it would be a good idea to revisit the library by yourself soon after such a tour, so that you begin to feel at ease there when you are alone. Choose a good place to sit and read, not near the door, where you will be distracted by other people, and not by a window if it's a warm day. Perhaps you can find a book which will give you a general introduction to study, as this one does, or a book which will provide a general introduction to your subject. Read for a short while, until you are familiar with the atmosphere of the building. Browse around to get the feel of the areas which will be of use to you, including computer and photocopying facilities. It will soon cease to feel strange.

In September or October, you may have a good deal of choice about where you sit in the library; as exam time approaches, you will find that there is little free space and a queue for any facility you need. More than ever, you will need somewhere else to prepare your assignments. This will probably be a room at home, in hall or in a shared flat. Make sure from the start that you have a space which is yours, and if you have to share a room, that you and your room-mate agree early on about times when there is quiet and when visitors are not welcome. You have work to do!

In order to concentrate, you will need a desk or table and a chair which is the right height for you. You will also need a good, directed light. Few central lights are sufficient for reading, and a small table lamp is essential. You may choose to have two chairs, one more comfortable, in which you can read, and another which is upright, giving you as much back support as possible when you are writing or using a computer. Physical discomfort is a great distraction.

For the same reason, it is not a good idea to work for very long stretches of time without a break. You will feel stiff, and your eyes will get tired. Plan your day, and include time for fresh air and exercise, after which you will work more effectively. Meet other students – not only those who are studying the same subjects – and join clubs and societies. Give yourself the sleeping time which is right for you – you probably already know whether you are a 'lark', working best in the mornings, or an 'owl', who works best late at night. Don't try to be both for long periods of time.

When you are working, you may like to have music to listen to, perhaps using a personal stereo. If this helps you to concentrate, it does no harm, but do remember that you will have silence in the exam room, and if you are too much accustomed to sound, its sudden absence can be unnerving. So do some of your work in silence, so that it always seems natural to you. For a similar reason, you should not always write with a computer; using a pen can seem strange and almost unnatural if you are used to a keyboard, and you will be writing by hand in your exams. You may also find that in this way you think more carefully of the exact message you want to convey; easy editing on the computer can result in careless writing.

During your study time, stop for short breaks, a cup of coffee for instance, and within your reading time, look up from the page or the screen every few minutes to allow your eyes to refocus: this will take only a few seconds, but it will help you to concentrate and to avoid eye strain.

Above all, try to keep to a regular pattern of work. If you get behind, it will be hard to catch up and you may start to panic as exams approach. Discuss your work with one or two friends, especially if you found some ideas difficult: if you all have the same problem, then go together to the lecturer concerned and ask for help – straightaway, not the day before the exam. Make a practice of handing in work on time; not only will this help you to get better grades as there may be a penalty for late work, but it also means that if there is an acceptable reason for lateness, such as being ill, you will meet sympathy and help rather than disbelief!

▶ First assignment

You will soon be given your first assignment, notes, an essay or similar. If you receive no guidance about its length, ask – it is much easier to plan if you know what the constraints are. It is also worth considering what the objectives of the lecturer are. Almost certainly, he or she wants to know how much you already know about the subject; it is not much use simply copying out your lecture notes. Can you think independently, give a reasoned opinion? Can you assimilate your notes and your reading, and have you taken the time to look up any reference which has been drawn to your attention? The lecturer is assessing you, not so much in terms of what sort of qualification you will get at the end of the course, but in terms of how much explanation the class as a whole needs, how familiar they are with the terms used, and perhaps what potential there is among the group.

This technique should be followed throughout the course, and in examinations. There is always a reason for setting a question, and it will pay you to try to see what that reason is. Look at the wording of the subject you were given: were you asked to discuss (see different aspects of the topic and assess them), to describe (factual, with less discussion), to analyse (work through stage by stage), compare, calculate? The wording will give you an idea of what is wanted, and, if you keep it in mind, you are far less likely to fall into the trap which is every lecturer's nightmare – writing all you know about the subject with no reference to what was asked for.

Writing or speaking in the context of student work has an in-built oddity: you are presenting information to someone who already knows. It is unlikely, although not impossible, that you will at this stage be truly original; you are not expected to have carried out research on the subject, as your lecturers have. Keep this in mind, as it will affect what you write: your lecturer does not expect you to be original, but you are expected to be reasonably thorough, using the information you have been given as a starting point, reading up extra details, if possible giving an example from your own experience, and assessing your material in a sensible and logical way. Presumably you chose your subject because it interested you; show your interest by being prepared to give your own opinion when it's appropriate; you may of course be wrong, but at least you will have shown that you can think independently.

You are unlikely to write in quite this way after you finish your education; in industry, you will write or present information to people who want to know, and who already believe that you are competent to tell them, otherwise they would not waste time reading your report or listening to your presentation. They may not be at all interested in your thought processes or calculations, but only in the results, and even then perhaps only in terms of benefits to the company and cost efficiency. But for this time in education, someone really is interested in why you think as you do and how you achieved your results, and it would be foolish to leave out such information when you write your assignments.

Nevertheless, there is a danger of overexplanation. Your lecturer knows the terms that are new to you, and you don't need to define them, although an indication of your understanding is a good idea. Some information will be self-evident, and some will come directly from the lecture; some students will simply repeat what they have been told, and the result is uninspiring to mark. Try to find your own example rather than the one given in class, comment on something that you have seen, refer to a recent article on the subject, and the lecturer will be only too ready to give you extra credit.

When you have gathered a sensible amount of information, and checked that it is all relevant to the subject you were given, plan a structure before you start to write. Later in this book, you will find help with writing and structuring notes and reports (see pages 27, 64), but even with your first assignment, you will need some kind of pattern to work to. There will be an introduction, in which you will explain how you have approached the subject, any limitations or constraints either in what you have been able to cover in the time or in obtaining the information, and, in outline, how you have organised your argument. Towards the end, you will have a summing up, assessing the overall impact of the material, giving your own opinion or perhaps agreeing with what others have written. In the middle sections, there must be a logical structure, in which you give any received opinion, look at different possible responses, consider any specific circumstances or examples, and then lead into the last section. You may use headings, as in a report, or you may be told to write in essay form, treating each section in a new paragraph: check exactly what you were asked to do. Then look at the length you were given, and in very broad terms decide how much space you will give to each aspect. When you have done this, you can start to write, leaving time to revise and check your work afterwards (see page 89).

I have assumed that your first assignment is a written one, as it is almost certain to be. However, even during your first term, you may be asked to use various methods of communication, and you therefore need to be aware of the differences of approach.

▶ Writing and speaking

There are obvious differences between conveying information in writing and presenting it orally, but both methods are important to you now and in your future work. Companies respond well to new employees who can both write and speak effectively, and your department will probably consider that these are important aspects of your learning process. Once upon a time, a scientist or engineer could hide in a laboratory or office and work in isolation, rarely if ever meeting customers or clients. This is no longer the case: from an early stage in your work as an industrial trainee, you may be in contact with a wide range of colleagues and with clients on whom the future of your company depends; whether you are marketing, designing, helping to manufacture or carrying out research, your ability to communicate well is as important as your technical knowledge.

Colleges and universities are increasingly aware of this, and include an element of communication teaching in scientific and technical courses. If you also consider such skills as important, and try to increase your own ability to convey information clearly and competently, you will gain credit in your course and at the end of it are likely to have more and better job opportunities.

A written document has particular characteristics: it can be a permanent record of work, although it may be updated from time to time; it can be transmitted, in hard copy or electronically, anywhere in the world, in translation if necessary; it is on the whole a one-way communication (in the past, it would certainly have been one way, but fax, e-mail and other such rapid means of transmission can result in an almost immediate exchange of views). Although any good writer has an individual style, there is little personality in a document; it cannot change itself because of the reaction of a reader who may be studying it years after it was written and far removed geographically from the writer.

On the other hand, a document may be read and reread over and over again, studied, discussed, analysed, annotated and shared with others. It can be as long or as short as the writer thinks appropriate, and it may contain diagrams or photographs which show fine detail, perhaps more than could be seen in real life with the naked eye. It can be the most suitable way of conveying detailed mathematical calculations or complex structures. Many of the assignments which you will produce while you are a student – and later – will do some or all of these things.

A presentation is a very different form of communication, by its very nature ephemeral and limited in scope. Your first attempt at a presentation will probably be as part of a group; even together, you are unlikely to be speaking for more than twenty minutes, and when you have finished, the occasion has gone for ever (assuming there is no video recording); it is no good having a bright idea five minutes after the end of the presentation.

Think about one of your lectures, especially one which you found clear and interesting. It lasted perhaps fifty minutes, and you spent much of that time trying to get down as much information as possible in your notes, to the extent that you may hardly have been able to take in what you were told. An audience at a presentation can't take notes in that way, and it would certainly find sitting still and concentrating for fifty minutes something of an ordeal. The lecturer has other advantages: he or she can come back to a point on the next occasion, refer you to an article or book for further detail, and even overrun by a few minutes if necessary, although this is not recommended. In a presentation, you have limited time and you must keep to it; the audience will make very few notes; you have to convey what you want to say then and there, to those who have turned up to listen. There is no second chance.

You will know, too, from your own experience, how difficult it is to take in details just by listening to them. Imagine a lecturer reading out a series of equations instead of writing them on the board! Think how little a good lecturer actually says in twenty minutes, and how little you could remember without your notes.

Writing and speaking are, then, two quite different methods of conveying information. Interestingly, you will find that within a company the same ideas may be conveyed in both ways, but with very different emphasis. The report is likely to contain all the detail, showing, for example, the tests to which a piece of equipment has been subjected, the results of the tests, the writer's reaction to the results, and various suggestions for the future, each aspect illustrated by diagrams and tabulated figures. How could all this possibly be conveyed in speech? The answer, of course, is that it isn't: in a presentation, the speaker would probably concentrate on the defects which were found in the equipment and the various possibilities of upgrading it, stressing those which seem to be the most suitable under the circumstances. The audience would be referred to the report if they wanted more detailed information.

You will need to keep this distinction clearly in mind. It will be important that you produce detailed work in your assignments, showing your procedures and your calculations as appropriate, but when you are asked to make a presentation, think again about what is really wanted. It is more likely to be in terms of the relative success or failure of your project, changes that could be made, opportunities for the future or applications of your work than in a detailed step-by-step analysis of everything that you did. Such information will be available in your report.

Later in this book, I will consider what makes an effective report and the elements of a good presentation, but this distinction between the two forms is an essential one if you are to communicate effectively in writing and in presentations during your course. Remember that in your document, you describe the nuts and bolts; when you talk to an audience, you say why the machine was needed.

Clearly, your objectives in producing an assignment, written or spoken, are of primary importance. Much of your work is involved with critical selection, of what you read (you can't read everything), of the notes you will record, of what you will write and what you will present. You can make a wise selection only if you know exactly what you are trying to achieve and why you are trying to achieve it, and it's always worth asking for clarification if you are not sure what is wanted. The need to identify your objectives is one which I shall come back to frequently in the chapters that follow.

▶ Key points

- ▶ Effective communication skills are an enormous asset both in education and at work
- ▶ Choose a place or places where you can work effectively, and make sure that you have a good directed light and reasonable physical comfort

▶ Develop a regular pattern of work; with exams in mind, practise studying in silence and writing by hand
▶ In preparing assignments, follow this pattern:
    check what is asked for
    read critically
    select appropriate information
    structure your ideas
    write!
    check what you have written
▶ Writing and speaking require a different approach and a different organisation of information

Part Two
Writing Skills

2 Listening, Reading, Making Notes and Taking Exams

▶ **Listening**

A wise ancient Greek, Zeno of Citium, said that we have two ears and one mouth so that we might listen more and talk less. He did not – as far as we know – add that we need to be trained to do both. Obviously, we start by listening, and only by hearing people talking to us do we learn how to speak, copying the sounds we hear and eventually mastering a language. Later, given the inclination and some ability, we may listen to different people and so master another language: we may try to do this from a textbook, but we will not become fluent until we hear the words spoken in a natural context.

Listening is, then, essential to our development, but most people aren't very good at listening. We tend to assume that it is a natural skill and that we don't need to be taught it: in reality, we often hear, but don't necessarily bother to listen.

Within further and higher education, you are called upon to do a great deal of productive listening, in lectures, tutorials and seminars, in conversations with staff and other students, and sometimes from prerecorded material, a video for example. It's worth considering what helps us to listen effectively, and what are the barriers that cause us to lose concentration.

Barriers to listening

An obvious area of distraction is physical discomfort. If the seat we're sitting on is hard or gives us poor back support, we tend to fidget and to be distracted; if the room is stuffy or the lighting poor, we find it difficult to concentrate. Background noise can be a nuisance, particularly if it's either loud and unpleasant (the grass-cutter outside the window) or too attractive (someone playing one of our favourite pieces of music). We can also find other people's conversations much more interesting than our own, especially if we hear our name mentioned – and it's interesting how we will hear our own name through a great deal of other noise and in spite of listening to something else. All these distractions may be outside our control, but if we take any opportunity to improve the situation (moving away from the window if the sun is in our eyes), we will be helping ourselves to listen less inefficiently.

Speakers can themselves provide distraction, and it's worth considering how they do this, not least to help us to avoid the same habits when we ourselves are the speakers. If the voice is too soft or too fast to be heard comfortably, we will simply stop making the effort (see pages 134–8 for advice about good speaking). Mannerisms can distract: we've probably all had the experience of remembering that the speaker took off and replaced his or her spectacles twenty-five times – we recall this long after we've forgotten the subject matter. A loud tie, ostentatious jewellery or totally inappropriate footwear makes us look rather than listen; if there is a clash between these two activities, looking nearly always wins. (I can still remember, after many years, hearing an otherwise professional presenter who, on a hot summer day, wore sandals and no socks but I've now no idea what he was talking about.)

Most of us, on occasion, suffer from a wandering mind. We can't help noticing how pretty the flowers are outside the lecture room window, and we start to daydream about our garden at home. We look forward, instead of concentrating on the present, either to the near future, thinking about our need for a cup of coffee after the lecture, or to the more distant future, wondering whether we shall manage to get a better vacation job than last year's, and then we start remembering how awful it was last year, how hard we worked for so little money and so on. It's all too easy and very human.

Positive listening

Can we prevent these barriers to listening? The absolute answer is probably no, but we can certainly listen more effectively than we often manage to do. Part of the art of listening well is preparation. If we don't know anything about the subject, or we don't know why we need to listen to it, we often imagine that it will be difficult to concentrate before we even start. Lecturers can help, of course, by telling us at the end of the previous week what they're going to talk about next time, and by starting the lecture with a quick résumé of last week's class and an introduction to what they are about to say, but sometimes we fail to listen to such help even when it's given. If we do listen, then we have the chance to read some background material, or at least to think beforehand what might be involved in the subject. Do we need this information because it's necessary background, because it's of general interest, or in order to be able to write about it in the examination? If we have some idea of the topic and the purpose of the lecture, we are far more likely to be able to concentrate.

We are also helped by taking notes. We shall discuss various forms of notes later in this chapter (see page 28), but apart from any other considerations, taking notes helps us to concentrate. We have to listen in order to know what to write. Of course we may occasionally go onto automatic pilot and write without really thinking, but it's hard to concentrate on one thing while you're writing about a different topic, and the physical exercise involved in writing tends to keep our minds active in the right direction.

There are other more dangerous distractions for a student, such as lack of interest. Some parts of most courses will be highly congenial, and other parts less so, but if we're going to do well in the examinations, we can't afford to switch off; in any case, we may find that the topic is more interesting than we thought if we listen carefully. As human beings, we are good at not hearing what we don't want to hear, and if we've decided in advance that the subject is boring and useless, then our minds are predisposed to finding something more interesting to think about.

As a student, you can also try to be more active in class. Asking questions is an obvious way to increase our interest and therefore our attention, but we can also give helpful signals to the lecturer. When we are talking, we know how important the audience's response is (see page 143 for a discussion of this point); if we lean forward, respond to eye contact, nod when we agree or look questioning if we're puzzled, an experienced lecturer will pick up the signals, and respond to them.

There will be pauses in the lecture, often to allow students to catch up with the note-taking. Use this time to think about the notes you're writing; try quickly to summarise the argument, or to foresee what is coming next. As you become more involved, you will find it easier to concentrate.

A clash of personalities nearly always makes communication more difficult. If you are listening to a lecturer you dislike for some reason, or who you suspect dislikes you, you will instinctively not want to listen or to respond. It's worth sitting down and thinking quietly about the situation, away from class. Have you a genuine grievance against the lecturer? If so, you need to talk to someone about it, and such discussion is outside the scope of this book. Is it something about the actual lecture which you're finding difficult? If so, do other people have the same problem? If they do, then it might be worth going as a small group to ask the lecturer to speak more slowly or to give more help or whatever the problem is. If it's simply a clash of personality, or, as sometimes happens, a dislike originating with someone else, the only answer is to respond in a professional way: it's a pity that this is happening, but it isn't the fault of the subject and it certainly isn't going to result in your getting a poor result in your exams; you will therefore do your best to listen attentively. This may be an occasion for enlisting the help of a friend in the class and discussing this aspect of the work together; this can be a useful way of generating interest.

It's possible to be too personally involved with the subject for easy listening. We can jump ahead ('I know what's coming next and so I don't need to listen'), or, more dangerously, we may prejudge the issue. We may have such strong opinions on the matter that we simply don't want to hear anybody else's theory. This is a highly unacademic attitude: if we want to study the subject in depth, we must be ready to hear all sides of the problem, and only then to make up our own minds. If we are too emotionally involved with what is said, we may spend the time planning our own response ('just wait till I can say what I think') rather than giving due consideration to the point of view being expressed.

Ideally, we concentrate on the speaker, reserving our judgement about the subject and making careful notes (see page 28). It isn't just a question of hearing and recording the words; we learn also from the speaker's tone of voice and the non-verbal communication employed (see also page 140). Lecturers may put forward a point of view in the hope that we will recognise its weakness; they may put forward a theory with which they themselves profoundly disagree; they themselves, being human, will have prejudices and may give us a partial or subjective point of view. If we are both listening and noticing the tone of voice used, we can often pick up such feelings, and they will guide us in our response. As students, you are not expected to agree with everything you are told, but you need a sound basis for your disagreement. Careful and critical listening is the first step. As the philosopher A N Whitehead said, 'A clash of doctrines is not a disaster – it is an opportunity.'

▶ Reading lists

You will probably not have spent long in further or higher education before you are given a reading list. It may look daunting; it may contain more material than you have ever had to read before. Don't panic. You aren't necessarily expected to read everything on the list: there may well be alternatives listed, for the very practical reason that there are far more students studying the course than copies of the relevant books in the library.

Lecturers tend to organise booklists into three sections. There are some texts which are absolutely essential to the course and every student is expected to have read them by the end of a set time. This is usually the shortest part of the list! You may think of buying one or two of these for yourself. There are two great advantages in this: you have a copy available whenever you want it, without having to join a queue for the library copy, and you can mark the copy as much as you like to help you remember the information for your exam. However, books are expensive, and there is the danger that you may buy a book for an immediate purpose and then not need it later – and the money has been spent. Ask the lecturer or your tutor for guidance; students from previous years of the course may also be able to advise you.

There will also be books on your list which are recommended background reading. You can probably be selective here, as several will almost certainly cover the same material. In the same way, books which are of general interest, the third category, can be chosen selectively, and also read selectively, a process which we will discuss later in this chapter (see page 23).

This advice is, of course, only general. Individual lecturers devise their own booklists in different ways, and you need to read your list carefully for clues about the relevance of various titles. Nevertheless, it's worth noting that every book in a booklist is not of equal importance to every other book.

Enjoy your reading. You have a wonderful, but limited, opportunity to read about the subject you have chosen to study; almost certainly, it's the only such chance you will ever get. The more you read, the more you will become involved with your work and the more satisfying it may well become. However, there are different ways to read, and it's essential to know how to vary your reading pattern.

▶ Reading skills

People read in different ways and at different speeds. Interestingly, the first research on eye movements in reading was carried out in France as long ago as the late nineteenth century. It was discovered that people's eyes don't move smoothly from left to right when they are reading; they move in a jerky way, 'fixating' on words for a fraction of a second. Some readers 'fixate' frequently, often rereading words, while others seem to take in a whole line of print while 'fixating' only two or three times. This is one of the major differences between fast and slow readers.

This book does not include a rapid reading course. Such courses exist, and can be helpful. However, there are various ways in which you can be guided to read more efficiently, which is very useful when you have so much to read. You may also find that you can read rather more quickly than you expected, partly with practice and partly because you have to a certain extent planned how you are going to read each piece of writing.

If you never become a fast reader, don't worry. There is no correlation between rapid reading and intelligence: some highly intelligent people are slow readers. The only problem is that if you read very slowly, you may lose an oversight of the whole passage; if you try to read a bit more quickly, you may concentrate more fully, and so remember more of what you read.

Preparing to read
Reading is a physical as well as a mental activity, and your physical wellbeing is therefore important to the efficiency of your reading. You will remember how reasonable comfort helps you to listen, and how discomfort distracts; it's the same with reading. Sit with the book at the right height for you, whether you're holding it or putting it on your desk or table. Most important of all, check that you have a good directed light – try not to sit so that the book is in your own shadow. If you have difficulty reading at the same distance as your friends, go to an optician and make sure that if you need spectacles, you have them.

Before you start to read, ask yourself some questions. What information are you hoping to get from this book (journal, report or whatever)? Why do you want this information? What do you already know about the subject, and so at what level do you need the information? Are you going to read for general interest, or because you need to memorise the contents?

We don't always read for the same purpose or, therefore, in the same way. You may be looking for just one piece of information, and the rest of the book is of no interest; you scan the pages in order to find what you want. You may want to check your own knowledge, and so you skim the pages, stopping only if you find a problem. You might be evaluating the book to see if it's worth reading, in which case you will probably dip into it here and there, spending more time on the contents page than on any other. If you need to learn the information for an exam, you will read more slowly, concentrating on each idea and maybe rereading extensively. The extreme of slow, intensive reading is perhaps checking proofs, when you are concentrating on each word, perhaps each letter, and I know from experience that in so doing, you tend to lose track of the message; it's possible to proof-read a book and to have only a vague idea of the content at the end!

There is a different type of reading, perhaps more appropriately called studying, which involves textbooks in maths, physics or related disciplines. It would be difficult to 'read' these books in the ordinary way, as each page may well be full of figures rather than words, equations rather than sentences. If this is true of many of your textbooks, you will know that you are primarily trying to understand and to make the methods used your own; you will probably be making notes and also trying things out for yourself: knowing this, you will need to have a pen or pencil, a notebook and a calculator beside you as you work.

So your reason for reading is very important, as it will affect the way in which you approach the task, and therefore your success or failure. It's very easy to waste time by choosing the wrong method of reading: we all know the problem of skimming a book to evaluate it and finding that the material is irrelevant to our needs but absolutely fascinating, so that we're still reading the same book half an hour later! This is most enjoyable, of course, but not recommended if we're in a hurry.

Reading critically

We have to decide what not to read. There is a tendency, often among bright, interested students, to try to read too much. Booklists need to be approached critically; we need also to have the courage to discard material because it isn't really what we need at the time. Of course we may go on reading out of interest, but if we have an assignment and limited time, it may be more sensible to make a note of what we'd like to read and to go back to it later. We may discard material because it's at the wrong level: there's always a temptation to read what we already know because it makes us feel good, but such reading may not be productive. If we find that the book is at too advanced a level, we perhaps ought to discard it or note it for the future and then leave it, because if we don't, we may become confused or disheartened.

We also need to allow thinking time. It's good that we have spent time in reading widely before we write an assignment, but if we don't have a chance to sit back and to consider what we've read, to assimilate it, to be critical, and maybe to come up with a new idea of our own, then what we write will be secondhand, worthy perhaps, but with little individuality. This thinking time also helps us to remember what we've read, as we're allowing it to become our own property, rather than just words on a page.

There is a temptation to believe what we see in print. This is very natural and, in that a book has been through a selection process by a publisher, it has some credibility but this cannot be relied on without question. Take the example of two newspapers of different political persuasions, published on the same day and recording the same events. Each has been selective, as they see different happenings as important or controversial. They may have different formats, which draw attention to (or hide) particular information; one may have pictures to make a story more graphic while the other uses the bottom corner of the left-hand page to make the same story less noticeable. The words will be different: the English language has a great many words which say more or less the same thing with different emphasis, and so one paper may find a story 'sensational' while the other finds it 'intriguing'; one may describe a particular politician as 'frank' or 'outspoken' while the other describes the same person as 'tactless' or even 'devious'.

This is an extreme example, of course; textbooks are unlikely to indulge in such rhetoric. Nevertheless, a book may be written in defence of a particular point of view, in order to attack a different point of view, or because of a passionate conviction on the part of the writer. A subject such as pollution, for example, can be treated in very different ways, and 'facts' can be produced to prove almost any point of view. If a book seems to have been written from the author's strong convictions, it's worth trying a book or an article on the same subject by someone else, to see if the message is different. Your lecturers may help in this by mentioning that a particular writer has a notable prejudice; information you were given in class might undermine the argument. Ask questions from your own general knowledge, and note whether the book gives you an answer. If not, can you guess why not? Reading critically makes the whole task more enjoyable.

Realistic reading

If you are reading a thriller on holiday, you may become so involved with the story that you read the whole book at one sitting. You will have forgotten most of it within a day or two, but that won't matter. If, however, you are reading material which you need to remember for examination purposes, you cannot afford to read in this way. Again, you must adapt your method of reading to the circumstances.

It would be unrealistic to try to read the whole of a textbook as you would the thriller. Concentration is short lived, and you need to use this fact to help you to read productively. Set yourself realistic targets, such as finishing a chapter or a section, or perhaps just reading a few pages. Stop when you have completed this, and take stock. Try to summarise what you have read; make notes on it, perhaps using more than one form of notes (see page 33). Ask yourself one or two questions on the basis of what you have read, to check your understanding and your memory. If your material is mathematical, you will need to be trying problems as you study. From time to time, allow your eyes to focus on some distant object, just for a moment, before you look back at the page, as this will help you to avoid eye strain, and will aid concentration. (It is useful to do this at regular intervals during your reading.) If the material is difficult, and you find it hard to concentrate sufficiently, bribe yourself with the promise of a cup of tea or coffee at the end of the chapter. A few minutes' break will in any case help to keep you going. When you feel that you have completed enough work for the day, be willing to forget about it for the time being, and go out to meet your friends. Next day, start by trying to recall the essentials of what you read the previous day; you will then be more likely to go on working with the positive attitude which will help you to remember.

Using the format

There will be a format to everything you read. Later in this book, I suggest some specific formats, for your notes, for reports and for dissertations; you will soon become familiar with some of these, and will be able to use them when you read such documents.

Many textbooks follow a pattern, although without the detail which a report, for example, might show. This format is helpful to you as you decide whether you need the book for general reading or study purposes. It's worth making a habit of using the following checklist for guidance in choosing books in the bookshop or the library; you may be prevented from making mistakes which are expensive in both time and money.

Assessing a book

- *Title*: the title of a book indicates its subject matter; it may also give a pointer towards its approach or level – 'an introduction', for instance.

- *Date*: the date when the book was published is of critical importance if it contains scientific or technical data which could have been superseded; unless you are carrying out a historical survey, most of your material will need to be recently published.

- *Preface*: this will probably tell you more about the author, including other books which he or she has written. Note whether any of them is familiar, through a comment by your lecturer, a review, or your own reading. You may also learn about the author's prejudices, and about the level at which the book is written.

- *Contents*: this is extremely important, and much of your scanning of a book will start here, whether you are looking for specific information or checking the coverage of the subject. Sometimes there is a useful short summary after the title of each chapter.

- *Introduction*: it's worth reading quickly through this, as it will give you a clearer picture of the author's purpose and the level at which the book is written. It will also indicate what is not covered in the book.

- *Chapters*: chapters have their own titles. These help you to find your way round the book and to read it selectively. In the case of other documents, such as reports or articles, there will be a system of headings which show you the way in which the information is organised, and its relative importance. You may well get a sense of logical progression through the material.

- *Individual pages*: using the index (see below), find a page which discusses a topic you are interested in. Skim read this page, glancing at the beginning of each paragraph and allowing your eye to pick out key words or phrases. If you decide to read the book, you will be at the mercy of the writer, and it's helpful to check if the style is encouraging. If it's written in a dense, clumsy or patronising style, you may want to think twice before committing yourself (especially to buying such a book).

- *Diagrams*: these often show you the level of the book; they can be a quick and effective way of conveying complex information. Equations and formulae are also useful indicators if you are assessing a mathematical book.

- *Index*: most textbooks have an index, to enable you to find specific details quickly and easily. It's also useful in helping you to decide whether the information is appropriate for your purposes: look up two or three topics, and see how much detail is given for each. Follow up one or two cross-references, which will show you more about the way in which the material has been organised.

- *Publisher's blurb*: there will probably be a short piece of writing on the back cover which tells you something about the book, its intended readership, and the author. This can be useful, but remember that its primary purpose is to entice you to buy!

Remembering what you read

Sadly, we all forget most of what we read. We are overloaded with information, nowadays on screen as well as in printed form, and our brains find it difficult to cope. If we are to remember what we read for examination purposes, we must employ techniques to help us to remember. Notes, which are discussed in more detail below, are the most useful technique, as the physical action of writing encourages us to remember, and in any case we have the notes themselves to go back to.

If you find a book in the library, or on a friend's bookshelf, you can't, of course, make notes in it. You may want to make your own written notes in the usual way, but if there are a few pages of special interest, it's worth photocopying them and then marking them up (see page 29) for yourself. (The law of copyright allows you to make one copy for your personal use.) Above all, make sure that you record enough about the book to be able to find it again later (again, see the section on taking notes, page 31).

Your friends are especially useful in helping to fix information in your mind. They are probably in two categories: those who are studying the same subjects, and those who aren't. Both are useful. Meet your class colleagues regularly, in small groups, and revise together, or discuss a particular lecture, or a book which you have all read. You may get a different perspective on the material, the discussion may itself be a pleasant experience, and you are confirming what you have read. If you hear a different and interesting piece of information, make a note of it as soon as you can, at an appropriate place in your notes.

Friends who are studying another subject can also be persuaded, perhaps on an exchange basis, to listen as you describe a topic which you are studying. They have no preconceptions, and are therefore more likely to see inconsistencies or an illogical argument. Sometimes an apparently 'simple' question from them can make you look at a topic in a new light, or clarify your thinking. You are then likely to remember the discussion.

There are techniques for helping you to remember specific facts, some of which you may have met at school. If you have, then don't hesitate to use them again. It doesn't matter if they seem rather silly, in fact, in some ways the sillier they are, the better. You may, for example, relate a difficult fact to an ordinary, everyday object; if you associate your fact with the kettle, then you will find that when you pick up the kettle to make coffee in the morning, the fact comes unbidden into your mind. Association is a useful way of helping us to remember what we read, which is why using a pattern or colour in notes (see page 29) is such a good idea – it's easier to remember a pattern than a great many words.

Reading practice
As with most skills, reading improves with regular practice. Try to make a daily routine for yourself of a certain amount of reading connected with your course. Apart from anything else, this will help you to keep your work up to date and to be prepared for future lectures. Don't limit yourself to this: read other material regularly, such as a newspaper or a magazine connected with one of your hobbies. As you read these things, practise varying the way you read. Skim some passages, summarise others as you finish them, try to read more quickly by allowing your eyes to 'fixate' on only two or three key words in a line, taking in the other words through your peripheral vision, and refusing to go back even if you feel that you've missed something. You will find that your general reading speed becomes a little quicker, and that you are more adept at varying the way in which you read. Be willing to slow right down to perhaps only a hundred words a minute, or even fewer, if what you are reading is complex, and to speed up to at least four hundred words a minute if you are familiar with what you are reading.

Read critically, not only to assess the usefulness of what you read, but also to improve your own writing style. If you find a passage or an article particularly easy, try to analyse why this is so, and what features of the writer's style have helped you. Extend your vocabulary by finding new words in what you read, and enjoy the challenge of trying to write more fluently yourself. Efficient reading and good writing style are advantages which last a lifetime!

▶ **Making notes**

Much of your time, while you are a student, is taken up with making notes, from lectures, books and journals, from CD-ROMs and the Internet. You will probably find that your lecturers take it for granted that you are competent at this skill; if you have had no help in the past, you may find it difficult at first.

This section will consider making notes from these different sources, and will give an example of how this might be done in practice. Of course, the application of these techniques will depend to some extent on your subject, and you may need to adapt these suggestions as appropriate. However, there are some guidelines which will generally be of use.

Know why you are taking notes before you start. You will have seen that I have made more or less the same point about starting to listen and to read: there is a great deal of emphasis throughout this book on the need to prepare thoroughly before undertaking almost any student activity. Much time is wasted by the lack of preparation, and if you don't think about your motivation for taking notes, as with other aspects of your course, you will find that they are less helpful than you expected.

We make notes primarily to help us to remember, but some notes are for immediate or short-term use, and others for use in the long term. Clarify your purpose: if you need notes just for a specific assignment, you may make them in an abbreviated form with indifferent handwriting, as you will be able to remember enough to make everything clear. If you are going to need your notes for exams in several months' time, you must be much more careful that everything is clearly written and all the abbreviations are explained. It's all too easy to be sure that you would never forget ... until you see your notes again a year later.

Your notes may be intended as general background reading, in which case they may be much less detailed than notes which must be memorised. Lecture notes are likely to be reasonably full, but should not include witty asides or jokes made by the lecturer in order to give the occasion a little light relief (although if the wit helps you to remember, there is a case for noting it, but not for repeating it in an exam paper).

Notes from lectures

Lecturers use a range of techniques, and you will soon become familiar with your lecturers' idiosyncrasies. You will also soon identify good and less good lecturers; if there are serious problems with the latter, such as speed or a tendency to mutter, you may want to go as a group to talk to the lecturer, or to mention the problem to your tutor. If the subject is new to you, you may wish to consider buying an introductory book of the 'Made Simple' type, in order to give you some background and help with unfamiliar terms.

Prepare for the lecture by considering what you were told on the previous occasion and calling to mind any clues given about the next class; practical preparation will include buying wide-lined A4 paper and drawing an extra margin at the right-hand side. You can then use the printed margin for headings or numbering (see below), and leave the new margin for later comments and additions – particularly important in the case of scientific or technological information which can go out of date even during your course. Apart from your normal pen, have one in a different colour, so that you can mark up anything which is clearly of importance.

Headings and numbering can be added to your notes later, as long as you leave space; sometimes the lecturer gives you a clue, by saying 'There are two aspects to this', or 'I'm going to suggest four different approaches'. A good lecturer will also provide headings, by making it clear when a new aspect of the subject is about to begin, or when a different point of view follows. The format you are creating will be very useful to you when you revise from your notes.

All notes, from any source, must be dated. As I have already indicated, information can go out of date, and it may be of great importance that you remember that you made your notes before a particular piece of legislation, for instance. Within each lecture, number your pages. The combination of date and page number will help you to keep all your notes in the correct order, which may be particularly important if, for example, you take out a few pages to lend to a friend who was ill and missed the lecture. Incidentally, if you do this, always make sure that you agree when the notes are to be returned and check that they are – you will need your own notes for revision purposes.

Some lecturers give handout material to their students. There are two advantages to this: you can concentrate on listening to the lecture as you will need to write less, and you can be reasonably sure that the information on the handout is accurate (and legible). The disadvantage is that it is easy to assume that because you have a handout, you know the information on it, without reading it. If you are to remember, you must make the handout your own, by marking it up after the lecture and adding comments from your own reading. It should also be dated and numbered along with your own notes.

As I said earlier, human beings are not, for the most part, good listeners. Don't assume that because something is clear in the lecture, or in your notes, that you will necessarily still understand it months later. For this reason, it is a good idea to go through your notes as soon as possible after the lecture, on the same day if this can be done. If you find a gap in your understanding, talk the problem over with colleagues or ask the lecturer at the next class. Add headings and numbering when you can. Underline or highlight points which you must especially remember. Rewrite your notes in a different format (this is also a good way of revising them). Colour-code each page, perhaps highlighting in red points which are important and in blue points which you want to look up later. You need to be able to remember this information later, and the colour pattern on the page will help you to visualise the content.

Nowadays, students sometimes wish to record their notes without the need to scribble frantically with pen and paper. If you would like to use a cassette recorder for the lecture – or if you need to do so because of a disability – courtesy demands that you ask the lecturer's permission first. It is unlikely to be refused. Recording the lecture has the disadvantage that you don't immediately have notes to mark up or revise from later, and a recording can easily be wiped out by mistake; you will also depend upon the lecturer's voice: if you try to record a lecturer who is given to walking around the room, you may have only a partial record of what was said.

Laptop computers are sometimes used for taking notes, and they have the advantage – provided the user can type quickly and accurately enough – of producing clear, legible notes. The two provisos are important, though, and if the note-taker gets tired or left behind, the record is not as helpful as it should be. Before you use any aid such as a cassette recorder or a computer, check the room to make sure that there is a power point nearby if you need it, and that the battery isn't going to run out before the end. Whatever equipment you use, notes should be printed out and marked up as soon as possible after the class.

Mathematical notes

The approach to a lecture in mathematics is slightly different from that in other subjects, because of the nature of the material. Some concepts have to be memorised (for example, that 8 is greater than 7), while others have to be understood (for example, that 308 is greater than 307). Everything in your notes which needs to be memorised should be clearly marked, so that it can be revised before examinations, and you need to check your understanding as often as possible. Notes are also important in order that information which was clear at the time can be recalled accurately later: for this reason notes should be taken on all appropriate occasions, not only at lectures but also at tutorials and from textbooks. A logical solution to an example may be perfectly clear when it is produced, but very difficult to recall.

It's particularly important that notes are taken accurately; a poorly written word might be guessed at, but figures or symbols must be clear. Practise writing Greek letters so that you can produce them quickly and precisely; you will need to copy down most of what is said in lectures or written on a blackboard, with comments added as appropriate.

Mathematical conventions must always be followed, such as the use of 'x' for the variable and '$\times$' for multiplication. Identify briefly how one step develops to the next, again using the correct conventions, such as $\therefore$ for therefore, $\because$ for because, 'iff' for 'if and only if', and so on. Check the usage in your textbooks if you are unsure about any of the conventions. Number equations on the right as (i), (ii), etc, and identify their use, for example 'Using (i) and (ii) ... '. If something is assumed from elsewhere, use 'we know that ... '.

Students of mathematics must listen with great care and follow the argument as well as taking notes, and good lecturers will allow time for this. If you lose the thread, ask for a recap at the time, and at least ensure that each step is written down with as many comments as possible in between, to help you later. Review your notes as soon as possible after the lecture, ideally writing everything out again, checking your understanding as you go, with textbooks available to help you if you find a problem.

Handouts help by reducing the amount you have to write, but be sure to add comments to show how one line is derived from previous equations; reference your handouts by numbering specific examples so that you can relate them to the problems in your notes. If you are using a textbook, copy out solutions line by line, trying out examples to test your own understanding, and making sure that you record the source (see below) in case you need it again; this is good practice for all note-taking from a published source.

▶ Recording information from printed sources

Much of your note-taking will be from books, journals and other published material, and it is essential that you record as many details of your sources as possible. There is an obvious practical reason for this, in that you may well need to go back to the information later to check it or for further details. It's enormously frustrating to know what the book you used looks like but to have forgotten the author's name.

There is an even more important reason for recording the published material you use. A book or article is the result of someone's thinking and experience, often of their research, and it remains their 'intellectual property'. If this material is used without credit being given to the writer, the property is in effect stolen, and this is as serious an offence as any other theft – especially in an academic community in which people's careers depend to a certain extent on their publications.

You will therefore need to indicate clearly when you use material published by someone else. You may quote exactly, in which case you need to show the extent of the quotation: if it is only a few words, put them in quotation marks (normally single quote marks); if you quote more than one line of print, start the quotation on a new line and indent that line and any subsequent lines of the quotation, so that the block of text stands out clearly from the rest of your writing.

There are two ways of giving the details of the work you are referencing. You can insert a small superscript number at the end of the quotation, and then give the full bibliographical details at the end of your work; this is a common way of showing quotations in books and articles. The second method is widely used in scientific and technical writing: at the end of the quotation, give the name of the author, the date of publication and a page reference in brackets and, as before, the full details at the end of the text. One advantage of this method (usually known as the Harvard system) is that there is no risk of confusion between a superscript number which refers to a quoted source and a superscript number which is used mathematically. There is a second advantage from the point of view of the person marking your work: the author's name will probably be familiar, and there will be no need to look up the full reference.

There are different conventions for setting out the information which you put at the end of your assignment or dissertation, and your lecturer may give you guidelines. The examples below are based on the Harvard method of referencing, and show common conventions which you can follow if you are not told to use a different form.

> Book reference: textual mark: (Brimblecombe, 1996)
> Note at the end: Brimblecombe, P. (1996) *Air Composition and Chemistry*, Cambridge, Cambridge University Press, 2nd edn.
>
> Part of a book: textual mark: (Crosby, 1996)
> Note at end: Crosby, N. (1996) The United Kingdom, in Adair, A. *et al.*, *European Valuation Practice*, London, Spon
>
> Article reference: textual mark: (Amos, 1982)
> Note at the end: Amos, B.J. (1982) Viability of *Pisum sativum* seeds at low temperature, *Annals of Applied Biology*, 97, pp. 243–428
>
> Conference paper reference: textual mark: (Hollis and Bright, 1999)
> Note at the end: Hollis, Malcolm and Bright, Keith (1999) Surveying the survey, in Hughes, W., ARCOM Fifteenth Annual Conference, September 15–17, 1999, Liverpool John Moores University, vol. 1, pp. 265–74
>
> Official publication: textual mark: (HMSO, 1996)
> Note at end: Great Britain, Office for National Statistics (1996) *Guide to Official Statistics*, HMSO

Note that when there are two authors, both are named, but if there are more than two, use the first named and then *et al.* (and others). There are various other Latin tags which can be used as you make up your list of references, such as *ibid* (the reference is to the same work as the previous reference) and *op cit* (the work has been referenced earlier), but unless you are confident in using them, they are generally better avoided.

You may wish to number your list of references at the end of your assignment, and perhaps to divide it into two or more sections. You will have used some general works as background reading, without actually quoting from them. These are, strictly speaking, bibliography rather than references, and it is usual to list them separately under this title. 'References' is then used for works which you have quoted from or used directly. You may also have a list of 'Unpublished sources', in which you can include unpublished works such as a dissertation or thesis by a previous student.

A moment ago, I mentioned using published work without actually quoting from it. You may want to refer to the results of someone's experiment, for instance, without actually quoting the words of the original. You are still using someone else's intellectual property, and it is essential that you show that you are doing so. The format is the same: when you have referred to the experiment, use the author's name and the date in brackets in exactly the way in which you would show a quotation, and again put all the details at the end.

There is a grey area in using references, and it can lead students into trouble. Some information which was originally the result of someone's research is now so well known that it can be said to be 'in the public domain'. The reference earlier to the research into eye movements in reading is in this category: most educated people know that a reader 'fixates' on particular words several times in a line of print; the fact has been used in print so often that there is now no need to give a specific reference. You will often see from your own general knowledge that particular information is in this category, but if you are in doubt, either ask your lecturer or give a reference anyway.

Using intellectual property which is not your own without referring to your source is very serious, and every student should be aware of the dangers of doing so. For this reason, you are strongly advised to put into your own notes immediately all the details of any material which you take from a published source. At the time, you will be aware that the material is not your own, but there is a risk that in a year's time you could copy it directly into your dissertation and forget that it wasn't yours originally. It is an easy mistake to make, but the consequences could be disastrous, for it would be very difficult to prove that you had no intention of stealing someone else's words. Develop the habit of noting your sources every time you gather information, so that there is no danger of facing this problem. It will also then be easy for you to build up your list of references at the end of your assignment.

▶ Formats for notes

As you make notes from books and articles, try to use headings and numbers in the way that was suggested for your lecture notes (see page 28). You have more time at the stage of actually writing the notes, and if you make them look clear and interesting by colour-coding them, you will find this helpful when you use them again later.

You are probably used to making notes on sheets of A4 paper used in the portrait position. There are other possibilities, which you may want to use when you are revising for exams. You will be going through pages of notes, taken from lectures and published sources perhaps over several months or even years. The notes will sometimes look heavy and uninspiring, and you may feel an understandable reluctance to spend time reading them over and over again. I have already suggested using colour to add interest and as an aid to your memory; you may also find it helpful to produce new notes in a different form. Summarise each page of your notes in a sentence or two, highlighting the most important facts; summarise several pages in a paragraph, again emphasising what matters most. You will find that the task of producing the summary itself helps you to remember, and the summaries themselves will be invaluable for last minute revision.

Your notes could also be reproduced in a more visually attractive way, as a 'spider diagram'. Turn a large sheet of paper on its side, in landscape position, and then write your main topic in the centre of the sheet. Now add subordinate information round the 'spider body', very briefly – preferably only two or three words at a time. Draw a circle round each piece of information. Now try to group the circles, either by drawing lines or by using different colours to make associations between various points which may have appeared in different areas of the page. You may also be able to add subordinate circles to your main circles, to show when a major point has perhaps two or three lesser facts associated with it. After a little while, you will find that you have a structure to your notes, and, if you feel it would be helpful, you might want to redraw the spider, now making all the connections clear.

It takes a bit of practice before you can draw a spider diagram quickly and easily, but if you try it out a few times, you will find that you can rewrite and organise your notes at speed. You will also have a great deal of material recorded in a small space, and if you draw the spider diagram on a large file card, you can carry material for revision in your pocket – each time you look at the spider, the circles will jog your memory about important facts which you need to remember. As you will see (page 70), I recommend this method of organising material for reports, dissertations and indeed almost all you write – and for your presentations, too.

It is easier to see this process than to read about it, and so I've given some of the information from the start of this chapter as a spider diagram in Figure 2.1. Later in the book (see page 72), I have used a further example of the use of a spider diagram in organising material for a report. Try it out for yourself, starting with information which is fairly straightforward, and you will probably soon be able to produce notes and organise your material in this way without difficulty.

▶ Notes from the Internet and similar sources

Nowadays, students are expected to take notes from computer sources as well as from the more traditional books and journals. There are, as with any other material, good and bad aspects to this: somewhere on the Internet, for example, there is probably most of the information you need; there is also a vast amount of other material, so that it can take a long time to find exactly what you want.

The scale of the problem is immense. One hour is 3600 seconds. If you can call up and scan a page in 20 seconds (which is quite speedy), in one hour you can see 180 pages. If you carry out a search and find a thousand references, it will take at least 10 hours to look at them all briefly and this doesn't include either the time taken to make notes, or pauses while you have something to eat.

Before you start on such an enormous task, therefore, it's wise to find the addresses of suitable sites from lecturers, colleagues or from your professional journals. There is another reason for this: there is currently very little control over what appears on the Internet, less than might be expected from a refereed journal or a reputable publisher. If you have any reason to doubt the accuracy of the information you find (accepting that the website of a known and respected organisation is likely to be reliable), take notes and cross-check them with other sources that you can trust.

Information on the Internet is temporary. This is an advantage, in that you can reasonably expect that it is up to date, but it's also a disadvantage, in that it may have disappeared by the next day, or even sooner. If you find something useful, either print it out or make notes from the screen immediately, as you may never get a second chance.

The decision whether to print out for later use or to make notes from the screen is largely a matter of the time available and the purpose for which you need the information. There is also a cost consideration: if you are charged for the time, it is almost certainly worth printing out useful screens and making notes later. Always note the reference on your printed page, and in your notes.

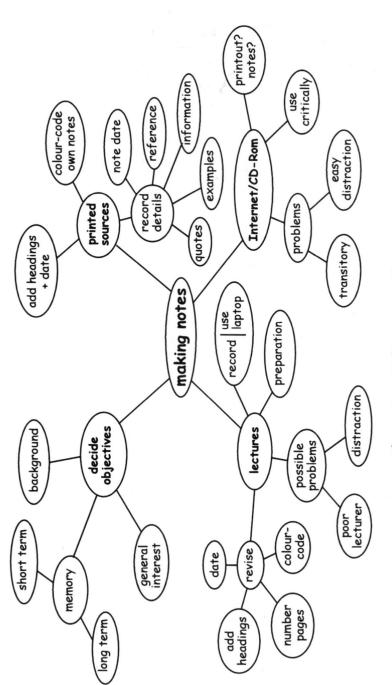

Figure 2.1 *Making notes spider*

Just because the contents of the Internet are so vast, there is an even greater temptation to be distracted than there is in a bookshop or library. You are almost certain to catch sight of information which seems much more attractive than the subject you're researching. Make a note of it, and then return to the subject which is your priority; you can go back to other topics when time, or money, permit.

Note-taking from CD-ROMs is more like using books and journals, in that the information is more or less permanent, and easily searched. The source and date of the material will be on the label, and should be used in your references. Again, you will need to decide whether it is better to save time by making notes from the screen, or to print the pages out and either make notes or mark up the pages later.

There is a huge range of information available to students nowadays; much of it is very up to date, especially that which comes by way of the computer. A book is nearly always at least a year, and a journal may be anything from one to six months, out of date because of the time taken by the process of publication, but a reputable textbook carries a weight of expertise which you can use again and again. All this material is potentially available to every student in your class, and it would be foolish to ignore such rich sources of knowledge. Your job is to be selective, and then to make the information you find usable by organising and assimilating it, often in discussion with your fellow students; it becomes your tool, but the job will be finished by your own critical thought processes.

▶ Exam techniques

Before the exam
Sooner or later, but in good time, you will have to start revising for exams. Your detailed revision plan will, of course, be dictated by your subject, but it's always worth having one, although don't spend so long in preparing a step-by-step breakdown of all the revision you will do that you don't have enough time left to do it. Working with a friend, draw up a list of the topics you expect to be examined on, study past papers and listen to any clues that might be given to you by your lecturers.

Different people revise in different ways: find the style that suits you best, but don't use only this one method – a little variety makes the task more interesting. You may talk out loud to yourself or to a friend, plan essays by drawing spider diagrams of the main facts, set yourself test questions or listen to a recording of your notes while you're doing a monotonous job like washing up. Don't overdo it, you still need both sleep and exercise, and a brisk walk in the open air helps to activate the brain!

Revise at least some of the time in silence, or you will get used to working with background noise, and in the same way handwrite some of your work if you are used to using the computer. Identify diagrams which you may have to produce during the exams, and practise drawing them at speed.

Shortly before your exams, check all the administrative details: where the exam will take place and how long it will last; the time it starts; the number of questions on the paper, and how many need to be answered; whether the paper contains compulsory questions, and how it is set out; the style of answer which is appropriate, for instance an essay, report, notes and so on. Make sure that you know what you are allowed to take into the exam room, such as the type of calculator, data sheets and so on. Check all this with a friend, in case you have misunderstood something.

During the exam

Immediately before the exam, you are likely to be nervous. Remember that most people feel the same, and most of them survive the ordeal. Don't, of course, take alcohol or drugs to calm your nerves, as they only slow your brain down. If you have to take prescribed medicines, check that they won't make you sleepy; if you are genuinely ill, tell your tutor or the invigilator before the exam starts; you may need a note from a doctor to confirm the problem. Before you enter the exam room, take a deep breath and release it in a controlled way, exactly as before a presentation (see page 135).

Read the exam paper carefully, and note the questions you are thinking of answering, adding one or two 'options' in case you have second thoughts. Allocate your time between these questions, remembering that you will need time to study them and think about your approach before you start to write. Make sure that you answer the question in front of you, and not the one you would have liked the examiner to ask. Allow a small amount of time for checking your answers.

Start with the question you like best, to give you confidence, but don't overrun your time limit. Always answer the right number of questions: it's worth remembering that the first five marks are easy to get, but the last five are extremely difficult. Don't waste time 'padding out' your answer; the time is better spent on another question.

If you have to answer a question you haven't prepared, don't panic. Sit for a few minutes breathing well and relaxing your shoulders, thinking about the topic, trying to remember lectures or something you have read, or discussed with friends. You will probably remember enough to get you started, and you may then be able to recall information you didn't realise you knew. This is the effect of nerves, which help you to think in an alert way, as long as you keep them under control. If you feel that there is more you want to say but your time allocation has run out, leave a space and come back to it later; if this brings you to the bottom of the page, write PTO so that the examiner knows there is more to come. If time is running out, you may need to answer your last question in note form; you may lose some credit for not writing it out in full, but you will gain from showing that you had the right ideas and only shortage of time held you back.

When each exam is over, put it out of your mind. Don't go endlessly through what you and your colleagues wrote – you can't change it, and you will soon start to feel that they have written better answers than you have, whether this is true or not. This doesn't help your confidence. Think positively: the next paper may be much better than you expected. Promise yourself a treat at the end of your exams, so that you keep your spirits up and have something to look forward to. There is life beyond examinations!

▶ Key points

Listening
- ▶ Try to avoid distractions such as physical discomfort and background noise
- ▶ Prepare to listen. Decide why you need the information and why it is important to you
- ▶ Take notes, ask questions and listen critically. Be involved

Reading
- ▶ Tackle reading lists in a positive way, and enjoy your reading
- ▶ Practise a variety of reading styles, and choose the right one for your immediate purpose
- ▶ Read critically, with realistic criteria
- ▶ Use the checklist on pages 24–5 to help you to assess books in the library or the bookshop
- ▶ Find helpful ways of memorising information, for instance by discussion or word association

Making notes
▶ Decide on your objectives before you start
▶ Notes from lectures: record useful information and mark it up after the class
▶ Mathematical notes: record accurately, follow conventions and check your understanding
▶ Notes from printed sources: record important bibliographical information so that you can reference accurately
▶ Vary the form of your notes, using patterns, diagrams and colour to help you to revise efficiently
▶ Notes from the Internet: be selective, print out if appropriate, record the source and date. Try not to be distracted

Exam techniques
▶ Identify your personal revision style, but vary the methods you use
▶ Revise sometimes in silence; practise drawing diagrams at speed
▶ Check the administrative details of the exam
▶ In the exam room, read the questions and allocate your time. Don't spend too long on the easiest question
▶ Don't panic! Think positively

3 Good Writing Style

As you read the articles and books recommended during your course, you will have noticed that the presentation and style of writing varies greatly. Some writers seem to discourage study by the very look of their pages, densely packed with information, in small print and with little margin space. You may also find that the writing itself seems unfriendly: one common effect of this is to make you reread sentences, not because they contain complex material, but because it's difficult to work out the meaning at once.

Other writing has the opposite effect: you expected to find the topic difficult, but as soon as you started to read, you were encouraged, first by the use of space and an attractive font, and then by the flow of the words and sentences, so that you were surprised how much information you absorbed in a relatively short time.

Your readers – at present mainly the staff who teach you – have exactly the same reactions. They have to read a great deal of student writing, and they naturally want the experience to be as rapid and pleasurable as possible. Nevertheless, they are under a professional obligation to tackle what you have written and to assess it. Later, when you are employed, the problem will be more stark: if your writing is going to take a long time and much dedication to read, nobody will. Your influence on your colleagues and senior managers will wane and promotion will pass you by. This might seem like exaggeration, but it isn't; the need to communicate clearly, accurately and effectively in writing has never been greater, and your scientific or technical skills will make little impact if you can't write well.

In this chapter, I shall look first at the need to be accurate, that is, to use the language in such a way that you make your meaning clear to your readers without ambiguity or uncertainty. This will involve using words and sentences in a precise way, and ensuring that the result is readable. There is a bonus for you in this: once you can use the language clearly and accurately, you will find that you achieve power over it, and that you can influence your readers just by the way in which you write. You will be writing effectively, and this is a rare and precious skill.

Having introduced this chapter as a guide to good scientific and technical writing, I must add that of course this isn't a basic grammar book; if you need the rules of punctuation and syntax, you will need a different book – perhaps one of those listed in the bibliography. I shall discuss ways of controlling your writing, and give specific examples of common errors to guide you.

▶ Appropriate writing

Writing has to have a context. There are few absolute rules for every style and every readership – you have to choose what fits the task in hand. If you are writing for a close friend, and the subject is an evening out, there are very few rules, indeed, your grammar may be slipshod and your punctuation almost non-existent, and it won't matter, as long as your friend gets the message. However, there is a limit shown in that 'as long as' – if the writing is so casual that the meaning is obscured, then your reader has a right to be irritated.

The style we shall be analysing in this chapter is appropriate for scientific and technical writing in most contexts. You may be writing a report or an essay, a dissertation or an article for publication: the way you write will have slight variations but it will essentially be similar. It will be clear and unambiguous; it will also be formal (the implications of this will be discussed later). In order to achieve this, you will need to use the rules in a way which hardly mattered when you were writing to your friend.

You will no doubt have noticed that in this book I don't apply all the rules for formal writing that I'm suggesting for you. This was a conscious decision. Before I started, I decided that because I spend much of my working life with students, I should try to develop a similar relationship with you, my readers, as with the students I teach. I hope and believe that there is a friendly and informal atmosphere in my lectures, and I have therefore adopted a similar style in the book – but on other occasions, when it's more appropriate, I write in a more distant and formal style.

I've stressed 'writing', as there are major differences between the way in which we use the language in writing and the way in which we speak. We'll analyse these differences more closely in considering the spoken language (see page 115), but it's important now to recognise that 'writing as we speak' is a difficult and unsatisfactory way of communicating.

When we speak, we use techniques which aren't available to the writer. Even a simple expression such as 'thank you' can be spoken in ways which suggest genuine gratitude, sarcasm, irritation at being kept waiting, condescension, disregard ... and no doubt many other states of mind. The meaning depends heavily on the tone used and the emphasis given. Tone and emphasis aren't as obvious in writing – we need to add other words, or describe our meaning more fully, or use artificial means such as underlining.

For these reasons, and others such as body language (see page 139), we convey our meaning more easily in speech; our grammar can become careless, we can jump from one sentence to another without completing the first, we can repeat details that we want to stress, and generally speaking it doesn't greatly matter. In writing, we have to express our meaning as precisely and concisely as possible, although we have one obvious advantage in that our readers can reread something if they didn't understand it the first time – but if they have to do this often, they may well give up in disgust.

Good writing in this context, then, involves using all the tools available in an accurate way in order to help and encourage our readers; we must keep both the needs of our readers and the purpose for which we're writing in mind. Our primary tools are words and sentence structure, and each will be discussed in turn.

▶ Words

Words: formal and informal

Earlier in this chapter, I wrote that scientific and technical writing is almost always formal; this consideration affects our choice of words. We are unlikely to address our readers directly as *you*; we are equally unlikely to refer directly to ourselves, and so *I* is rare; *we* meaning the members of the group (or company) is sometimes appropriate (for further discussion of this point, see report and dissertation writing, page 76). Unless there is a good reason for doing so, we should not write:

> I've carried out the experiment and will tell you the results as soon as I've analysed them.

It's more appropriate to write:

> The experiment has been completed, and the results will be made public after analysis.

Another good reason for avoiding the personal in our writing is that a personal style tends to be more diffuse and rambling, removing emphasis from the important information, as in:

> I must point out the anomalies found in this investigation.

which has more impact if we write it as:

> There are anomalies in this investigation.

Two words which should be avoided because they are too casual and too ugly for good writing are *done* and *got*; it would have been possible to write:

> The experiment has been done and when we get the results, they will be made public.

but no good writer would do so. Experiments are carried out, and the results are obtained.

You will have noticed that the first (informal) example includes the abbreviation *I've*; this is very informal, and so is appropriate in speech or casual writing, but not in the style we are describing. Always spell out such expressions: use *do not* rather than *don't*, *shall not* rather than *shan't*, *it is* or *it has* rather than *it's*. In the same way, use the full word *laboratory* rather than the common spoken form *lab.* and *diagram* rather than the not uncommon written abbreviation *diag.*

Formal writing is always accurate. In Chapter 4, I look at the need to use the correct forms of, for example, the names of laws or the abbreviations for units (see page 87). It's also important that you give precise details as far as you possibly can, and this means that you should hesitate to use vague expressions such as 'a lot of', 'quite', 'relatively frequent' (relative to what?), or 'more often' (than what?). Ask yourself whether you can give a figure, or a percentage, or relate to a known fact to clarify your meaning.

Words: jargon

Some words are part of your professional jargon – terms which you use regularly in your work, but which are less common in ordinary writing. Watch out for these expressions, and decide how far they are appropriate for your readers and the context in which you are writing; you can't avoid them and shouldn't try to do so when you're writing your assignments, but realistically you must make a decision about how far your readers are familiar with the terms you use (for a further discussion of this point, see pages 75–6).

There is, however, a different kind of jargon which you should always try to avoid. It tends to be wordy, it's probably a cliché, and it will irritate your readers. The most famous example is *at this present moment in time*, meaning *now*, but other expressions become fashionable and are then overused in a similar way. *Basically*, for example, can have a useful meaning ('this is basically a simple question, but has been made to sound complicated ... '), but it is often used carelessly, in much the same way as 'actually' ('this is actually the right style' means no more than 'this is the right style').

Words to be used with care

Words are often used carelessly, in spite of the fact that they can affect the meaning. I'd like to look at a few examples which are often found in student writing. *Then* is often added to a conditional expression ('if you press the switch, then the light comes on'); it is perhaps intended to stress the sequential nature of the action and its result, but it also suggests a passage of time rather than an instantaneous effect. In the example given, the reader might query the length of time which might elapse before the light went on, and how long a time should be left before any remedial action is taken. If 'then' is omitted, readers will take it for granted that the result occurs virtually at once.

There's another bad effect of the overuse of 'then': it can produce boring writing, for example:

> Each cylinder was then cut into discs 2mm high. The discs were then divided into six groups, then placed on dry filter paper and then weighed.

The repeated use of 'then' adds nothing to the meaning, and has a dulling effect on the whole passage.

A far more dangerous word is *only*. This little word influences the nearest word or expression, and as a result its position can change the meaning of the whole sentence:

> This equipment is available to order and for this term will cost a thousand pounds.

If we add *only* to any point of the sentence, we shall change the meaning: 'this equipment only ... ' means that no other piece of equipment is in this category; 'is available only to order' means that it has to be ordered; 'for this term only' means that the price will change after this term; 'will cost only a thousand pounds' suggests that it's cheap at the price. If only is placed carelessly in a sentence, the whole message can be distorted; it must be kept close to the words it influences.

There's one other problem with 'only', and that is its use in casual speech to mean 'but', as in:

> I'd like to go, only I don't think I can spare the time.

As long as we use the word in this way only when we're speaking, it isn't likely to cause misunderstanding, but strictly speaking it's inaccurate, and so should never be used in writing.

Groups of words can become confused and so cause misunderstanding. Three awkward combinations are *less/fewer*, *amount/number* and *greater part/majority*. In each case, the first expression (*less, amount, greater part*) is used to describe variation in one single object or idea, as in:

> There was less work involved than I expected.
> The amount of carbon remaining was very small.
> The greater part of the time was spent in preparation.

The second expression in each case (*fewer, number, majority*) is used when there are several objects or ideas involved, as in:

> The increased use of pesticides has resulted in fewer butterflies than there were twenty years ago.
> The number of students studying physics has declined.
> A majority of those interviewed wanted to work in the financial sector.

Interestingly, we can think of less as qualitative (qualifying the amount of work) and fewer as quantitative (a measure of the number of butterflies). The distinction between these words should be kept in mind, as the meaning of the sentence might depend on their accurate use: the distinction between less important qualifications and fewer important qualifications could be critical!

Words: American usage

In English, we sometimes use a difference of spelling to show the use of a word: *practice* with a 'c' is a noun while *practise* with an 's' is a verb. This *c/s* distinction isn't always made in the same way in American English, which tends to use the 's' form more freely (our *defence* is *defense* in American). There are too many differences to be discussed here, but you will notice that in English, as opposed to American, *program* refers specifically to a computer program while other kinds of programme, for instance at a theatre, are still spelt in the traditional way, with 'mme'. If you use American English for some reason, you will need to be consistent: *centre* will be written as *center*, *colour* as *color* and *travelling* as *traveling*. Generally, it's better to keep to the form of the language which is natural to you. It doesn't matter whether you spell words such as *organise* in this way or as *organize*, but again it is essential to be consistent.

Words: singulars and plurals

Spelling is always a problem in English: words come into the language from many sources, and so are formed in different ways (for example, Latin 'a' endings become 'ae' in the plural, as *antenna* becomes *antennae*, although in industries which use the words frequently, the Anglicised form *antennas* is not uncommon). Spelling rules themselves are often cumbersome and hard to remember, or have so many exceptions that it hardly seems to be worth the effort; perhaps the old saying 'i before e except after c, as long as the sound is ee' is one of the few which are sufficiently useful to be learnt.

It's important, nevertheless, to be able to spell words and to use them accurately when they are common in our own area of work, and we shall use them regularly. So we need to know that *spectrum* is singular and that the plural is *spectra* (similarly *stratum/strata*); the singular *phenomenon* has the plural *phenomena* (similarly *criterion/criteria*); buildings have *roofs* and multiple *storeys* – both plural words which are frequently used incorrectly. As you read textbooks and articles for your assignments, you will see such difficult words correctly used, and it's worth making a note of, and learning, any which you might often write.

Words: new developments

Languages aren't static; they change in response to many kinds of influence, and they expand with the development of new ideas and technology. As a result, you may find yourself unsure about the suitability, or the form, of new expressions. After all, the word *mouse* used to make people think first of a small furry animal! Sometimes adjectives are used as nouns: people will speak of a *floppy*, or a *remote*. If you wonder whether to use such words in your writing, check in a recent journal from a major institution in your field of study – it's likely to be setting the standard. Similarly, many new words consist of two old words brought together, and this is how they are mostly written – *database*, *online* and so on but check if you are unsure. Dictionaries, even the one in your computer, can be out of date (useful though they are for most purposes).

Some new inventions are both ugly and unnecessary. A student recently wrote:

> This allows re-useability and up-gradeability.

which is, in its way, perfectly clear, but nasty. It's just as easy, and far more readable, to write:

> This allows [the product] to be reused and upgraded.

▶ Punctuation

Before we move on from words to sentences, it's worth looking at the main forms of punctuation as they are used in formal writing. Accuracy is just as important here, for poor punctuation can affect the reading, making comprehension difficult or creating ambiguity. Good punctuation, on the other hand, guides the reader through the information and adds considerably to the ease and pleasure of reading.

We use much less punctuation than we did in the past. This is partly the effect of wordprocessing – saving keystrokes means saving time and therefore money – and partly a desire to simplify the language. Sometimes this doesn't matter; for example, whether we indent paragraphs or punctuate addresses is no more than a matter of taste or convention. At other times the punctuation is critical to the meaning, and to leave it out is a crime against the accurate transmission of scientific and technical information.

In this section, some of the most common types of punctuation are described, with a short example in each case, and a comment on any particular problems with usage.

Full stops

Full stops are one of the simplest and clearest forms of punctuation. They appear at the end of a sentence (for the definition of a sentence, see page 55), and are followed by a capital letter at the start of the first word of the next sentence.

Full stops used to appear in abbreviations, but do so much more rarely nowadays. Most people write *etc* and *eg* without full stops. (For a more detailed discussion of abbreviations, see page 87.)

Colons and semi-colons

Colons and semi-colons are different pieces of punctuation, but as they are often confused, it makes sense to treat them together. The primary use of the full colon (:) is to introduce a list, whether it is written down the page or, if it's short, along the line. So we may write that some of the main forms of punctuation are: full stops, colons, semi-colons and commas. In a scientific report, we might find 'Earthquakes produce two kinds of waves: P waves and S waves.'

A longer list which is written down the page is treated in the same way, except that it probably won't have internal punctuation such as commas; a final full stop is useful in clearly identifying the end of the list, especially if it coincides with the foot of the page. The example which follows shows how the list may be set out and punctuated:

> Major hazards in the research laboratory include the following:
>
> Correct use and storage of solvents
> Removal of solvents on rotary evaporators
> Correct use of vacuum systems and high pressure systems
> Use of cryogenics and the condensation of liquid oxygen
> Disposal of pyrophoric residues.

If the items in a list are themselves long enough to be separate sentences, use the colon to introduce the list, and then normal punctuation, as in:

> Some of the advantages of enzymes are given below:
>
> They are specific in their action and are therefore unlikely to produce unwanted byproducts.
> They are biodegradable, and therefore do not cause environmental pollution.
> They work in mild conditions, that is, at a low temperature, neutral pH, and normal atmospheric pressure. They therefore tend to be energy efficient.

I've dealt with lists in some detail because they are very useful to the writer; it's easier to think your way clearly through the information if you list rather than use a long paragraph, and it's certainly easier for the reader to absorb the information in this form.

The other principal way in which you are likely to use a colon in your writing is as the introduction to a quotation. You will notice that all the indented examples in this book have been introduced by colons; every time that you quote a sufficiently long passage, that is, a line of print or more in length, set it out in this way and use a colon. (See also the note on references, page 32.) Equations are introduced by a colon in the same way, the equation itself always being on a separate line.

Semi-colons are very strong punctuation – almost as powerful as, and sometimes an alternative to, a full stop. They should therefore be used sparingly. If two ideas are closely linked, by a logical connection or perhaps a contrast, and they would normally be written as two separate grammatical sentences, a semi-colon can be used to bring them together. They become two equal parts of one sentence (there's no capital letter after a semi-colon), and the connection between them is emphasised, as in the following example:

> The larvae of the Death's Head Hawk Moth are not uncommonly found on potato plants in England; the insect, however, cannot survive the English winter.

Commas

Commas are the hardest punctuation to discuss, as their use often depends on the sensitivity of the writer rather than on hard and fast rules. There are, however, occasions when a comma is essential if the reader is to understand the sense of the sentence. If we write:

> The sentences which were written under examination conditions were confused and ungrammatical.

we are saying that of all the sentences available, those which were written under examination conditions were distinguished from the others by being confused and ungrammatical. If, on the other hand, we put commas round the words 'which were written under examination conditions', we link these words to 'the sentences'; we are in fact describing these sentences. So if we write:

> The sentences, which were written under examination conditions, were confused and ungrammatical.

we're saying that all the sentences we're talking about were written under examination conditions and therefore had the undesirable features. We can see how serious this distinction can be if we think of the difference between

> The tests carried out at high temperature were conclusive.

(which suggests that those which weren't at high temperature were inconclusive) and

> The tests, carried out at high temperature, were conclusive.

(which suggests that all the tests were carried out at high temperature and so were conclusive).

You will probably have noticed that introductory expressions often take a comma, to show that they are a comment on the sentence that follows rather than a major part of it: *In this case*, *As you see*, are in this category. Other 'comment' expressions also have commas: *that is,* in the middle of a sentence, or *on the other hand*.

Commas are also used to add information which is said to be 'in apposition', that is, an extra piece of information added to words which themselves form a major part of the sentence. So we can say:

Professor Jones, Head of the History Department, has written a new book.

in which case we are adding information about Professor Jones immediately after his name is mentioned. Another example might be:

The heating system, installed last year, has already proved its worth.

In each case, the extra description ('Head of the History Department' and 'installed last year') is enclosed by commas; you will notice that if you read these sentences aloud, you will naturally pause in the places marked by the commas.

This is the point at which the discussion of commas becomes less precise, and the writer's feeling for the flow of the language takes over. Most fairly long sentences (perhaps more than about 20 words, although it's impossible to be precise) have a pause built into them – when you read them out loud, you will probably pause and perhaps take a breath at these places. In writing, a comma marks the pause. Probably the easiest way to find out where to put such commas is to read the sentence aloud and notice where your voice wants to pause. This isn't an infallible guide, but it's a useful one all the same.

Later in this chapter (see page 55), we discuss how long a sentence should be and the problems of overlong sentences, but it's worth stressing here how useful commas are in guiding the reader through the text, showing how sections of a sentence belong together and are separated from other developments of the idea. You have just seen this process in action: my previous sentence contained 53 words, which means that it's rather long. It contains:

- introductory words (later in this chapter)
- a reference in brackets (see page 55)
- an informative section (we discuss … overlong sentences)
- a second informative section (but it's worth stressing … through the text)

- a development of the ideas (showing how ... the idea).

It would be difficult to read and absorb so much information in one sentence if it weren't for the commas, and you will notice how they occur at each transition point within the information.

Notice in your own reading how such commas help the flow; be careful in your writing not to put commas where they interrupt the flow, as in:

> The mechanical part of the load cell, was fully tested.

when the meaning suggests one flow of words through the sentence. If you read this sentence aloud, you are unlikely to pause after 'load cell'.

Apostrophes

Of all the punctuation in the English language, it's probably fair to say that the apostrophe causes most difficulty – so much so, that some people simply ignore it altogether. This is not sensible, however, as it can show whether a word is singular or plural, and this may be important to the meaning. Its absence also makes the text look casual and perhaps careless; if the student hasn't bothered to use apostrophes, perhaps it's because he or she has a poor grasp of the language as a whole.

Apostrophes aren't as bad as they're painted, once you grasp the principles. One of their uses is to show where a letter or letters have been omitted, for example *don't, can't, wouldn't*. The good news for the scientific or technical writer is that such expressions should always be written out in full, as *do not, cannot, would not*, and so there is no need for an apostrophe at all.

This is even true in the most contentious case of all: *it's*. This means *it is*, or *it has* (it's time to hand in the assignment; it's been a long term), and under no other circumstances does the word ever have an apostrophe. In scientific and technical writing, you will always write *it is* or *it has*, and never 'it's'.

The confusion is caused partly by the other use of the apostrophe, which is to show possession. This is the case in which the singular or the plural is so important; 'the student's failure' (one student has failed) needs to be carefully distinguished from 'the students' failure' (more than one student has failed). Only the position of the apostrophe will reveal the difference of meaning.

If you remember these principles, you won't go wrong with the apostrophe. One of the two most depressing sights for a lecturer (I speak from years of experience) is to see ordinary plural words with apostrophes just because they end in *s*, even though there is no suggestion of a letter omitted or of possession. The other is to see the word 'its' with an apostrophe!

Hyphens

As with commas, so with hyphens – we use fewer that we used to, and this often causes no problem at all. However, we can't dispense with hyphens altogether, partly because they can affect the meaning and partly because they can help the reader to understand easily and quickly what we mean.

In scientific and technical writing, a hyphen can show us how to interpret the information: we read and identify the concept almost as if it were one word. So, the words 'stand-alone', and 'look-up (tables)' are much easier to read than if each word was written as a separate entity.

Hyphens are also helpful in showing the reader how to join words together. There can be a string of words describing a substance, some of which are closely related to each other, while others are separate aspects of the description. The modern habit of omitting hyphens between the related words results in readers having to work out the connections for themselves; this may not in itself be a difficult operation, but it interrupts the flow of the reading and is therefore unhelpful.

A few examples will show how the use of a hyphen aids the reading:

    a cross-section of students
    heat-tolerant micro-organism
    quasi-geostrophic theory
    particle-rotation
    aphid-resistant

Brackets

On the whole, brackets are best reserved for information which isn't an integral part of the sentence, as in the following examples *(see Figure 3.4)* or *(see Appendix A)*, and for abbreviations. The traditional way of introducing an abbreviation is by writing the term out in full on the first occasion on which it's used, and putting the abbreviation in brackets afterwards. After this, the abbreviation can be used by itself (but see the comment on abbreviations in Chapter 4, page 87). A typical sentence in a report might read like this:

> The wave files were stored in an Erasable Programmable Read Only Memory (EPROM) and played through a Digital to Analogue Converter (DAC).

After this introductory sentence, the terms EPROM and DAC would be used alone.

There is an entirely different use of brackets which will be useful to you in writing a thesis or similar document. Square brackets are sometimes used in quotations, when, in order to make the words quoted understandable, you need to add something to the words you are quoting. This happened earlier in this chapter, when I was discussing the ugliness of some modern word forms. I quoted the words 'reusability and upgradeability', and showed how the idea could be conveyed in better style as:

> This allows [the product] to be reused and upgraded.

The problem for me as a writer was that I didn't want to identify the product for reasons of confidentiality, but I couldn't write the revised sentence easily without doing so. The solution is to add words in square brackets: you know, and I know, that we wouldn't really write the words 'the product' in the sentence – we'd name it – but the convention of square brackets solves the problem.

You may find that as you use quotations, you often need to add a word or two in square brackets at the beginning of a sentence in order to make sense:

> This [the experiment] was carried out under climatic conditions which might invalidate the results.

Other punctuation

Other forms of punctuation, such as exclamation marks and question marks, are used comparatively rarely in formal writing, indeed, if you find that you are using them often, you may need to think again about your style. It's a good idea to avoid the dash as punctuation – it tends to take the place of commas, as in this example – both because it's informal in itself, and because you may be using hyphens and minus signs, with which the dash could be confused.

As I suggested earlier, a useful check on your punctuation is to read a passage of your writing out loud; if you find that you want to pause at exactly the point at which you've used punctuation, you are probably right, but if your voice is constantly stumbling over oddly placed commas or stops, you need to rethink what you are writing.

▶ Sentences

Before I discuss how sentences can be misformed and misused, I need to stress that a sentence must make sense by itself; we might not fully understand it without its context, but we should see that it contains a complete message. If we remember that, then it's obvious that the following aren't sentences:

> As more data are gathered every day.
> With reference to the previous experiments.
> For the following reasons.
> As detailed below.

In formal writing, we must always write in sentences which are complete and correct; if we're simply writing notes, we can of course write incomplete messages, as long as we're sure that we'll understand them later, but as soon as we're writing for other people to read, we must be sure that our sentences will stand by themselves.

Sentence length

A sentence can be too long for easy reading for two different but related reasons. It may contain too many words or too many ideas. Either fault causes problems for the reader. When we read complex material, we instinctively look out for a full stop, in the knowledge that we can pause at that point, reread if we have to, think about the implications of what we've read, or even ask advice if it seems appropriate. If we find that we're looking over several lines of print with no obvious place to pause, we start to panic, and either add our own full stop, not necessarily in the right place, or give up on the sentence and move on, hoping that all will become clear later. Neither is a desirable response.

For this reason, a sentence which is difficult in itself, because of its scientific or technical content, needs to be reasonably short. As an average, such sentences should be about 17 to 20 words in length; good style demands that we vary the length of sentences, but none should exceed about 40 words without a very good reason. Even this may be too long; if the sentence has several different ideas in it, it may be difficult to read and understand even though in terms of the word count, it isn't particularly long, as in the following example:

> The decay heat, without sufficient coolant, can rapidly raise the core temperature, with the possibility of severe core damage and the possibility of meltdown and the release of radioactivity.

This sentence begins sensibly enough, but after the word 'temperature', it presents us with three possibilities, each dependent on the one before. The awkwardness of this is shown particularly by the repetition of 'possibility'. If there is a full stop after 'temperature', the second sentence, now shorter, can simply read:

> This can result in severe core damage, possibly leading to meltdown and the release of radioactivity.

Overlong sentences are far too common in student writing. They are not only difficult to assimilate; they often include grammatical mistakes and ambiguity which compound the problems for the reader. If you keep your sentences short, but allow for some variation of length, you are likely to write more accurately as well as in a more readable way.

Sentence structure

Even in a comparatively short sentence, it's generally true that the first few words make more impact on the reader than later words. For this reason, it's generally a good idea to put the main point of a sentence at the beginning. I said 'generally', as there are times when you deliberately don't want to stress a particular point, or when you might choose to give the reader a surprise by withholding a major idea until the end of a sentence. Such occasions are rare; mostly, we know which point we want to stress and will therefore put it first. The difference of impact can be seen in the following example:

> A rare orchid was seen during an otherwise uneventful field trip.
> The field trip was uneventful apart from the sighting of a rare orchid.

In the first sentence, the rare orchid is stressed; it makes an immediate and strong impact on the reader. In the second sentence, stress is on the uneventful nature of the field trip; the orchid appears at the end almost as an afterthought.

Similarly, a sentence gains from having a strong beginning; in the following example, the writer has begun in an inappropriate, personal way, with no impact; the improved version has two emphatic words ('one diagram') leading into the detailed information:

> I have used all of the flow representations to create one diagram.
> One diagram contains all the flow representations.

If the flow representations are more important than the single diagram, this could be written as:

All the flow representations are contained in one diagram.

You will notice that the sentence gains if unnecessary small words are left out: 'all of the flow representations' can be written as 'all the flow representations'. It's easy to add words almost without noticing, as in: 'We carried out the experiment and the results we obtained showed that...'. If we carried out the experiment, then of course we obtained the results, and the words 'we obtained' can be omitted. It's always worth looking at your writing style to see if you have used many such expressions which can be left out without loss of meaning.

Sentences can begin in one construction and change to another halfway through, because the writer hasn't thought through the message before beginning to write. Two typical examples are:

> This method has both advantages as well as disadvantages.
> The reason for the failure of the experiment is because the students used contaminated materials.

The first writer could have said 'both advantages and disadvantages', or 'advantages as well as disadvantages', but trying to say both at once is clumsy as well as ungrammatical; the second could have said either 'the reason is that ... ' or 'failure occurred because ... '; whichever construction is chosen, it must be used consistently.

Infinitives, split and otherwise

The infinitive of the verb is its name: we identify the verb 'to be' or 'to read' or 'to think' by using the 'to' form. The two words that make up the infinitive (for example, 'to' and 'read') belong together, and on the whole it's bad style to split them by putting other words in between. So 'to thoroughly read' should be written as 'to read thoroughly'. However, we occasionally want to stress the word that describes the verb (called an adverb), and in this case, we can be forgiven for putting it between the parts of the infinitive, provided that we do this very rarely, and for a clear purpose. So we could accept 'to apprehensively read' (expecting to find the book impossibly difficult) if the writer is deliberately trying to take us aback by the use of the word 'apprehensively'. The rule is probably: don't split an infinitive by accident.

Interestingly, a sentence that begins with the infinitive of the verb is usually awkward to read, and better turned round, as in:

> To ensure that the results are valid, the researchers need to choose their data carefully.

which would be more logically ordered as:

> The researchers need to choose their data carefully in order to ensure that the results are valid.

Singular and plural agreement

If the subject of the verb is singular, the form of the verb must also be singular; in the same way, a plural subject must be followed by a plural verb. Difficulties often arise when there are several words between the subject and the verb, as in:

> A range of frequencies were selected
> A wide spectrum of particles were produced

In these examples, the problem is made worse by a plural word coming between the subject and the verb: so the plural 'frequencies' has distracted the writer from the true subject, 'range', which is singular; in the second example, 'spectrum', the subject, is singular, but the writer is too conscious of the plural word 'particles'. The examples should read:

> A range of frequencies was selected
> A wide spectrum of particles was produced

Beginnings of sentences

The first few words of a sentence, as I've said, have more emphasis than what follows. This impact is lost if too many sentences start in the same way – a common problem in reports, when there is a great temptation to write:

> First, we ... Then we ... Then we ... Finally we ...

This is boring to read. Try to vary the beginnings of sentences, so that the reader's attention is held.

I've highlighted some common mistakes and, I hope, given you some ideas for writing effective sentences. Read critically, especially textbooks by acknowledged experts in your field of study, and you will see ways of expressing complex thoughts clearly and succinctly for your readers.

▶ Paragraphs

Essentially, a paragraph contains a single 'story', that is, the information which belongs to one incident, description or result. In practice, this is difficult to manage. We may have too much material which belongs together, or we may feel that for the sake of the reader, we need to break up the text. Lists are described elsewhere (see page 49); they are often a more convenient way to handle information than long paragraphs.

Otherwise, we may simply need to break a paragraph after about half a page, using a few connecting words to show the relationship of the new paragraph to the old: 'At the same time ... ', 'On the other hand ... ', 'Under such circumstances ... ' are typical of these logical links; apart from their work in connecting pieces of text, they guide the reader towards what follows.

▶ Active or passive?

A great deal of scientific and technical writing is in the passive; this is sensible, but we need to be aware of the effect on our writing of choosing active or passive. First, the terms must be defined. A simple sentence – 'I tested the equipment' – starts with the subject, 'I'; it then contains a main verb 'tested'; finally there is the object 'the equipment'. This form of the sentence is called the *active*. If we turn the sentence round so that we start with the object, we are using the *passive* form: 'The equipment was tested by me.'

Even in this short example, we can see one of the differences: I, as the subject, gets a good deal of stress in the active form of the sentence; 'by me' seems almost superfluous at the end of the passive form – we might well leave it out. It's generally true that in using the active, we stress the subject, while in using the passive, we tend to neglect the subject altogether.

Traditionally in scientific and technical writing, we have used the passive deliberately, to keep the style impersonal and removed from us as researchers. In company terms, this has the additional bonus of removing our individual responsibility – 'it is recommended' doesn't identify the person recommending in the way that 'I recommend' does.

This is still a good principle, and in line with what I said earlier about avoiding 'I' and 'you' in formal writing. However, it's worth noticing other effects; active and passive are well named, as the active form is more direct, concise and strong in impact; the passive is more diffuse, longer, and comparatively lacking in impact. We choose which form to employ in the light of convention, our readership, and the effect we want to achieve. As a general guideline, use the passive in your writing unless you see a good reason for changing.

▶ Tenses

In speech, we move from tense to tense with little problem: 'I worried about the essay we're writing all yesterday, but now I'm writing it, I don't think it'll be too bad.' This comment starts in the past, moves to the present and ends in the future, but it's all clear to the listener.

In writing, we have to be much more careful about changing tenses, as the reader doesn't have our facial expression or our tone of voice to help. Most of our writing is likely to be in the past tense: we are reporting on work which we have completed. Occasionally, we may change to the present to make a statement which continues to be true ('Enzymes have an optimum temperature'), and if we need to suggest future developments, we will need either the conditional ('If time permitted, it would be interesting to check these results further') or the future ('This will have serious implications for all future research in this area.').

As a guideline, use the past tense unless you have a good reason for changing.

▶ Inclusive language

In the past, most people wrote as if the readership were exclusively male, as in:

> The reader would have expected a different result if he had had prior knowledge of the substances involved.

This is no longer acceptable. Nevertheless, you will want to avoid the cumbersome 'he or she' as far as you can, although, as I have found in writing this book, it's sometimes difficult to do so. On the whole, the plural will solve the problem ('Readers would expect ... if they ... '); sometimes using the passive will help, or restructuring the sentence, but if occasionally you are forced to use 'he or she', nobody is likely to query it, as, after all, you are showing your awareness of the need to use inclusive language.

▶ Listening to language

We can tell a great deal about language by hearing it. From time to time, choose a paragraph which you wrote a few days ago, and try to read it aloud. You will soon notice if your punctuation is in the wrong place, or if you've repeated words in an awkward way (good style doesn't allow repetition of a word within a line or two, unless the word is so specific in meaning that there's no alternative), or your sentence is so long that you run out of breath or your voice doesn't know where to go next. It's much easier to hear these problems than to see them on the page. If it's easy to read what you've written, and it sounds as if it flows well, you have the enormous advantage of being able to write in a way which will attract your readers. As I said earlier in this chapter, good writing is always appropriate to the readers and to the occasion.

▶ Key points

- ▶ Choose your style according to your readers and the context in which you're writing
- ▶ Scientific and technical writing must be clear, unambiguous, and in a formal style
- ▶ Choose your words with care, and spell them accurately
- ▶ Use punctuation correctly to clarify your meaning, give emphasis, and guide the reader through the information
- ▶ Keep the length and structure of sentences under your control
- ▶ Use lists rather than overlong paragraphs
- ▶ Use the passive form unless there is a good reason, such as clarity or impact, for the active
- ▶ Write in the past tense, unless you need the present for writing about a continuing state of affairs or the future for writing about what will happen later
- ▶ Don't offend your readers by using sexist language

4 Writing Reports and Dissertations

During your course, you are likely to be involved with three major assessed areas of writing. Early on, you will be preparing reports on the basis of material given to you in lectures, or noted in your lab book or logbook as you carry out experiments or use the workshops. You will almost certainly have had experience in writing such reports at an earlier stage of your education. Later, you may be involved in longer, more complex reports, especially project reports which record your work during a lengthy project lasting perhaps a whole term.

Towards the end of your course, you are likely to produce one final extensive piece of writing which will count towards your examination results: this may be in the form of a project report or dissertation. In either case, read carefully the information about layout and style given to you by your department; this chapter gives general advice, but clearly can't deal with all the variations which individual departments or faculties might require. There will also be regulations laid down by your university or college, and these must take precedence over any other advice you may receive. Nevertheless, there are basic features of reports and dissertations which it's useful to understand.

▶ Report writing

Writing reports is likely to be an integral part of your course, whatever your subject; it will continue to be an important activity when you leave education and start work. Almost every part of your job may give rise to a report: you may need to write a progress report to record the work you are currently involved with, and to produce a final report when the task is completed, both to justify the work you have done and to leave a record for other people; you may want to pass information on to colleagues or perhaps to other parts of your organisation; you may have to report the findings of your research so that they can be assessed for commercial potential; if you have visited a different site or another company on behalf of your employer, you will record the details of your visit so that your manager can see what has been accomplished; if you want to persuade senior colleagues to allow you more time, staff or facilities for your project, you will have to justify your request in a report. Reports are often exercises in persuasion, not just because you need resources but also because you want support, agreement or acceptance of your conclusions or the actions you have recommended.

These are just a few of the circumstances that give rise to reports; because they are so widespread and so influential, it's important that you practise writing effective reports at an early stage in your academic life. Inevitably, you will also find that you spend much of your working time reading other people's reports, and it's useful to be able to assess them, and to have clear criteria by which you judge whether the writer is making a good case or not.

Reader goodwill

The principal aim of almost every report is to achieve reader goodwill – to make readers feel that, whether they agree with the writer's conclusions or not, they have been presented with a thoughtful and balanced document. Reader goodwill is achieved in three main ways: the appearance of the report should be professional, encouraging the reader to look further; the organisation of the report should be clear and easy to use; the writing itself should be accurate, unambiguous and concise within the limits imposed by the subject matter. This chapter will look at each of these aspects, although not in this order. I have chosen instead the order in which you are likely to work, looking first at the structure, then at the writing, and finally at the presentation of your document.

There are also three basic aspects to the way in which reports are organised. In practice, a report may have many sections, as shown later in this chapter, but essentially a report writer introduces the subject, presents evidence and then comments upon that evidence. This is an underlying format on which you can build whatever structure is appropriate for your subject, your material and your readership.

Identification of the reader

The identification of your readers is the first and principal activity involved in preparing a report. You will need to know who your readers are, what their level of knowledge is and their experience of the subject, what they already know about your particular topic and what they need to know. At work, you may be faced with a common and difficult problem: writing one report which has to influence both technical and non-technical readers.

Fortunately, this problem is unlikely to arise while you are in education. You know who is going to read – and mark – your work; you know roughly what their expertise is, and also that almost certainly they will already be very familiar with all your material and your ideas. It's likely to be the only time that you will write in this way, using material which the reader knows even better than you do; outside the educational process, people read reports because they want information or ideas, not simply in order to find out whether you, the writer, know what you are writing about.

As a result of this peculiarity, you will need to think about your reader or readers in the light of their reasons for asking you to write this particular report. What will they expect you to include? What information will they expect you to find for yourself (will they check partly by looking at your bibliography?) and what will they expect you to consider and then reject as irrelevant to your topic? The last thing that any lecturer wants is for you to prepare an indiscriminate 'all I know about' answer; you show your maturity in part by deciding what it's appropriate to include in the light of the subject you were given, and what you have decided, rightly, to leave out. Some of your material may already be in your lab book or logbook, and you will have to show how you use the record you made earlier, selecting what is suitable for the present purpose.

▶ Structure

As with any assignment, look carefully at the information you have been given. You will have a topic, probably some comments for your guidance, and, especially at an early stage, a set of headings which you are expected to use. You may also be given guidance about whether or how you number these headings. Different subjects handle reports in slightly different ways, and you need to take note of the detailed guidance you are given: for example, in technical subjects such as engineering, the summary is always at the beginning, while in the pure sciences there is commonly an abstract at the start, stating very briefly what has been accomplished, and a summary at the end.

The structure of a report, then, will depend in detail on your subject of study and its particular conventions, and these must always be kept in mind. Nevertheless, what follows is a general format which is common to many reports, and which probably underlies the detailed structure you are given.

- *Title page* – The title page identifies the report, its writer, subject and date. Other information such as the writer's department or supervisor's name may also be included. The date is very important, as it shows the last opportunity you had to change or correct your work; any material which became available only after that date is outside your control.

- *Contents list* – The Contents list shows the overall structure of your report, and will therefore be useful to the person who marks it: if your headings show an appropriate and logical organisation of material, your report will almost certainly be given a good mark. You need to include the number of each section, its heading and the page reference, in that order, left to right.

- *Summary/Abstract* – As I mentioned earlier, the position of the Summary is dictated largely by the conventions of your subject. Wherever it appears, it should include a brief introduction to the topic covered, the most important aspects you have included and, very briefly, your main conclusions and recommendations, if there are any. A scientific Abstract states briefly the author's work and the main points of the results.

- *1 Introduction* – By convention, the Introduction is the first section to be numbered (check whether it's appropriate for you to number your headings). As its name suggests, this section introduces the topic of the report, gives any necessary background, and any constraints you may have been given, for instance a time limit. You may also discuss briefly how you have approached the subject.

- *2 [specific heading]* – The number of sections in which you present your evidence will clearly depend on how much you have to give. You may need to include evidence obtained from books and journals or from computer-based sources, all accurately referenced (see page 32), details of experiments you carried out, interviews you conducted, workshop activities – whatever information you need in order to make the case you are presenting. This is all evidence, and so should be given as impartially and impersonally as possible (see also page 76). A scientific report will probably have the methods and results sections at this point.

- *[number] Conclusions/Discussion* – In a report, there are Conclusions, not a Conclusion. You are not drawing your report to a close, but assessing the implications of the evidence you have already presented. This section is inevitably subjective, but it should be written as impersonally as what has gone before. Check that a Conclusions section is asked for and, if appropriate, number it within your numbering system. In a scientific report, the results will be discussed; there may also be a Conclusions section, but this is not always separate.

- *[number] Recommendations* – If a Recommendations section is required, then at this point you can suggest what action may be taken in the future. This may be in terms of what you would like to do, if time and your supervisor permit, or it might be a suggestion for any future students who might want to follow on from what you have achieved. It might even be a 'commercial' suggestion as to how your project could be developed in a profit-making enterprise. A scientific report might well omit this section.

- *Appendix or Appendices* – As you gave your evidence, you might have wondered how to handle information which for one reason or another, didn't fit, for example, computer programs, detailed statistics, long series of tabulated figures, which would seriously interrupt the reading if they were placed in the text. These can comfortably go into an appendix or a number of appendices at the end of your report. Appendices are often given letters, to identify them as separate from the main text.

- *References* – At the very end of your report, you will give all the bibliographical details of any material you have quoted, referred to, or used in any way, and which did not originate from you. Use one of the conventions for presenting references (see page 32 if you are given no guidance about this).

This is, as I said earlier, a general format which you will need to adapt according to the conventions of your subject and your department. Nevertheless, as you will see later (pages 68–70), it underlies most report structures which you are likely to be given.

Numbering systems

The question of numbering headings in reports is one which needs more comment. All reports have headings, but all headings are not necessarily numbered, although, as I said earlier, in some disciplines such as engineering, convention dictates that a numbering system is used. There are two main systems which are widely employed in industry, and it's useful to be familiar with both and with their advantages and disadvantages.

Paragraph numbering comes in two forms: either every paragraph in the report is given a sequential number, regardless of headings, or, more commonly, there is a sequence of headings under which each paragraph is numbered. So, if you have a main heading numbered 3, the paragraphs which follow will be numbered 3.1, 3.2, 3.3 and so on. This system has the advantage that if you need to identify a detail within the report, for instance over the telephone, it's very easy to locate the paragraph in which it occurs. The disadvantages are that the logic of the report's structure is limited, and that if you need to use subheadings, you will have to repeat numbers, so that subsection 3.2 is numbered in the same way as paragraph 3.2. This method of numbering is probably better avoided if you have a choice.

The second system, which is also widespread and avoids some of the problems of paragraph numbering, is known as *decimal notation*. According to this, headings and subheadings are numbered, but paragraphs aren't. So the main section 3 has subsections 3.1, 3.2, and so on, each of these having its own heading. The principle of decimal notation is that headings and numbers always go together. This allows a detailed logic in the structure: subsection 3.2.1.4 is clearly identified as being the fourth comment under 3.2.1, which itself is subordinate to 3.2, which is the second subsection in the third main section of the report.

I'll use the various aspects of a report which we're looking at in this chapter as an example of how this system works:

1	**INTRODUCTION**
2	**FORMAT**
2.1	**Headings**
2.2	**Numbering systems**
2.2.1	Paragraph numbering
2.2.2	Decimal notation
3	**WRITING STYLE**
3.1	**Choice of words**
3.2	**Sentence structure**

and so on! You may be relieved to know that many reports need only two or three levels of heading, and that none, however long, is likely to go beyond four levels.

You may be told which form of notation to use; if not, you will probably find decimal notation a more helpful system. In spite of its name, incidentally, it isn't a true decimal system: if you happen to have eleven subsections within the second section of your report, the last two will be numbered 2.10 and 2.11; if one of them itself has subsections, you may have 2.11.1 and so on. There is no limit to the number of subsections that are possible, but if you have too many, you may need to use more subheadings. As a very general guideline, if you have two consecutive pages without a heading of any sort, you are probably not using enough headings to guide the reader through your material.

There is also the risk of using too many headings. This has the unfortunate effect of producing a very cumbersome numbering system, as unnecessary levels of headings and notation reduce relatively important issues to subheading or sub-subheading status. Very often, this happens because of the repetition of headings, as in the following example:

2   BASIC PRINCIPLES AND USES OF OPTIC FIBRES
2.1 Basic principles of optic fibres
2.2 Uses of optic fibres

The main heading, 2, could be omitted, and headings 2.1 and 2.2 upgraded to main headings. No information would be lost, and two major topics would have the main headings appropriate to them.

Headings in reports

Earlier in this chapter, I said that, once the readership and the objectives have been ascertained, there were three main aspects to the preparation of a report: the structure, the writing and the presentation. It's very important that organising the structure comes first. If you try to organise your material and to write at the same time, each activity is likely to get in the way of the other, and you may find yourself scrapping all that you've written and starting again at quite a late stage – a terrible waste of time from your point of view. It's much better to take time to organise your material, and if possible to get your supervisor's approval of the structure you choose before you start to write. That way, organising and writing are separate stages, and, although it may seem to be substituting two activities for one, you may well find that the whole operation takes less time than if you make several false starts.

How do we do this? You already know the general format of a report (see pages 65–6), and you may have been given a list of headings which you must use. This will depend on your subject, but we can look at a couple of examples. If your subject is biological sciences, and you are preparing a report as a result of some experimental work, you will probably have headings like these:

Introduction (probably including the Aim, very briefly)
Method, or Methods and Materials
Results
Discussion
Conclusions

As you will see, these headings correspond roughly to those suggested earlier: the Aim is included in the Introduction; Method, possibly including a record of the apparatus used, and Results form the evidence section; Discussion is part of the Conclusions. This pattern holds good even if the list of headings is expanded, for instance to:

Aim
Hypothesis
Introduction
Theory
Apparatus
Procedure
Results
Discussion
Conclusions
Sources of error
Summary
Bibliography

As you can see, headings are rarely 'standard' in the sense of never to be changed; if for a good reason you need more headings or different headings, adapt those you have been given but be prepared to justify what you have done.

A different area of study may produce a very different set of headings. Suppose you are studying engineering, and have been asked to design a product. You may be given the following headings – almost certainly numbered:

SUMMARY

1 **INTRODUCTION**

2 **DESIGN PHILOSOPHY**

3 **IMPLEMENTATION**

4 **PERFORMANCE ANALYSIS**

    4.1 Description of tests

    4.2 Results

5 **CONCLUSIONS**

6 **RECOMMENDATIONS** *(if there are any)*

7 **REFERENCES**

Again, the basic pattern is the same: the Introduction and Design philosophy are both introductory material; Implementation and the Description of tests present the evidence; the Results and Conclusions are your assessment of the evidence, and Recommendations may be made if they are appropriate.

The lists of headings given above are in an order which is unlikely to be changed; they may also provide you with enough headings for the whole of your report. However, in a longer document you may need further headings, for instance Implementation might be subdivided into Mechanical work and Electronic work; the Results might be grouped according to different stages of the testing procedure; Recommendations might be both immediate and longer term. In each case, subheadings would make the pattern clear. All your headings and subheadings should, of course, be listed at the start of your report in your Contents list.

If you are writing a report which doesn't fall clearly into any of these formats, and you haven't been given any headings, then remember the basic pattern of Introduction, Evidence and Comment, and use a technique by which you can organise your ideas. In Chapter 2, the idea of spider diagrams was introduced; you may find that such a diagram is an ideal way in which to group your ideas and suggest suitable headings. Jot down your ideas and the material you have collected, and then look for connections and a logical order. Try out several possible formats to see which you think is the best for your purpose, and ask your supervisor's advice if you aren't sure. If you can get a good format at this stage, the writing of the report will be very much quicker and easier. You may want to use a spider diagram for one individual section of your report, as well as, or instead of, for the document as a whole. An example will show how useful this can be.

Introductions, as I've said, are notoriously difficult to write. In this example, a physics student wants to write the introduction to his design project report – he has designed a type of needlescope, a form of endoscope used in the treatment of eye problems. Even before he starts, he knows some of the aspects he will need to include – what an endoscope is (and specifically what a needlescope is) and why it's used, what its advantages and disadvantages are, a brief note of its history, and what he wants to achieve in his project. This, slightly developed, is the basis of his spider diagram, as you can see in Figure 4.1.

During the preparation of later sections of his report, he adds details as they occur to him, so that his spider diagram develops in the way shown in Figure 4.2. When he is ready to write this section up, he can decide on a logical order for all this information. As each aspect is written up, it's crossed off the spider diagram so that at the end, the writer has no doubt that everything necessary has been included.

As you turn your outline or your spider diagram into a sequence of headings, you need to make sure that they are appropriate for your readers. First, keep them short and helpful. Few headings are likely to be longer than four or five words, but those words must guide the reader to the content of the section below. The Contents list, which is where all your headings come together, is the nearest thing to an index that most reports contain. Your readers will use the headings in this way, as a means of identifying and locating specific material. If information is given under an inappropriate heading, it's effectively lost – you, as the writer, know that it's there, but the reader doesn't. For this reason, vague headings such as Miscellaneous, General or Further Information are unhelpful; because readers don't know what information is contained in such sections, most won't bother to read them.

Second, think about the form of your headings. Whether they are numbered or not, it's useful to the reader if they are in a clearly defined hierarchy. Use bold type for your main headings, as it stands out well on the page (but don't underline it, which spoils the effect). You may wish to use bold capitals for your main headings, and bold lower case for second level headings; this means that if you have a third level, you can simply stop using bold at that point, as in the example above (see page 70). Whatever the system you adopt, be consistent throughout the document.

You may choose to indent your subheadings, as in the engineering example. This can look attractive on the page, but mustn't be carried too far. If you have four levels of heading and indent further every time, you will in the end be writing in a narrow column at the right-hand side

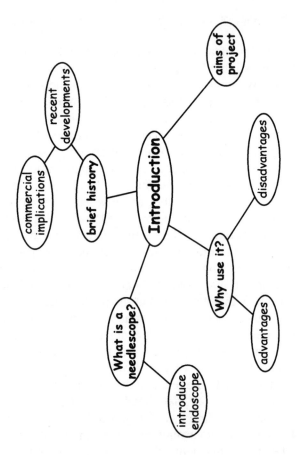

Figure 4.1 *Basic spider diagram for project introduction*

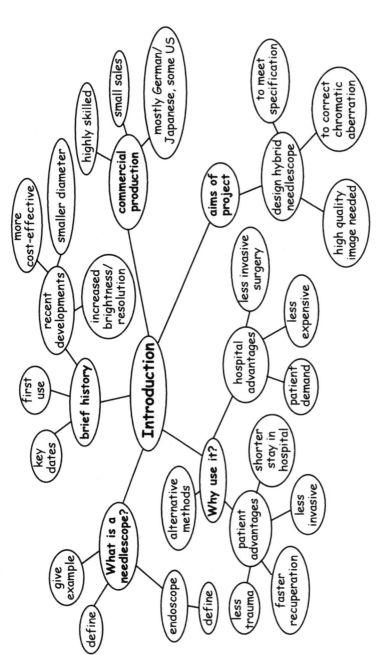

Figure 4.2 Final spider diagram for project introduction

of the page – meanwhile wasting a good deal of paper. It's probably wise to limit the indentation to the first subheading level and to keep the same position on the page for any subsequent levels of heading.

Third, think about the form in which you write your headings. Every word in a heading used to have an initial capital letter, as in **Description Of Tests**. This now looks rather old-fashioned, and it's better to capitalise only the important words, as in **Description of Tests**. Indeed, the modern tendency is to capitalise only the first word, as in **Description of tests**, but it's a matter of taste whether you want to go as far as this. As before, it's essential that you are consistent in whatever format you choose for your headings.

Lastly, headings, numbered or otherwise, need to stand alone. The numbers don't need brackets or any other decoration, and the headings themselves don't need punctuation (the only exception to this would be a question mark at the end of a question, but it isn't good style to use a direct question as a heading in any case). The text always begins on a new line under the heading, and shouldn't depend on it. The following heading is incorrectly used:

> **2.2   The Sodium Coolant**
> This allows the heat energy produced ...

The correct version would be:

> **2.2   The Sodium Coolant**
> The sodium coolant allows the heat energy produced ...

Reports can be, and often are, judged in the first place by the quality of their headings; it's worth getting this right before tackling the next stage of report preparation – the writing.

▶ Appropriate style

Once you have decided on your format, you can begin to write your report. Don't feel that you have to begin at the beginning, not least as the Introduction is a notoriously difficult section, and you may sit for so long in front of your PC that you lose enthusiasm for what you're doing. Choose a section of your report which you feel will be relatively straightforward, such as Apparatus, and start with that. You will feel much better once you've made a start, and as you already know your format, you know exactly where your section is going to fit into the whole.

Reports are formal documents, and if you've already studied Chapter 3, Good Writing Style, you will know how to write in an appropriate style. There is no point in repeating all the good advice given there, but it can be summed up, as it applies to reports, in the following twelve guidelines, which you can use as a checklist whenever you write a report.

Checklist for report writing

1. Keep your sentence length under control (maximum 35–40 words in a sentence)
2. Keep your paragraph length under control (not more than half a page in a paragraph)
3. Use logical connections, such as 'therefore' and 'moreover' accurately
4. Follow the conventions of your subject for abbreviations, signs, symbols and so on
5. Don't become personal, emotional or chatty in a report
6. Don't address the reader directly as 'you'
7. Avoid referring to yourself, especially in the singular 'I'; 'we' may sometimes be acceptable
8. Don't use abbreviations such as can't, it's, don't
9. Use formal, precise language rather than expressions such as 'fairly slow', 'a lot of equipment', 'the write up in the lab book'
10. Write as concisely as possible, and avoid waffle
11. Use clearly identified diagrams, acknowledging the source as appropriate
12. Check all you write, including any corrections you have made

---

Most of the points summarised above have been discussed elsewhere, but a few need to be looked at further in the context of reports.

In point 4, the use of symbols and abbreviations was introduced. Many scientific and technical reports include a great many of these, and it's obviously important that you follow standard usage in your subject. However, you may need to use abbreviations which will be unfamiliar to some of your readers even if they have some knowledge of the topic you are writing about, and this suggests the use of a Glossary. In company terms, a Glossary also gives you the chance to explain abbreviations which are widely used within your organisation but not known outside (almost any large organisation is likely to use such expressions).

Obviously, your lecturers are likely to be familiar with the symbols and abbreviations you use, but it isn't a bad idea to get used to including a list of abbreviations, in alphabetical order, in your report. A Glossary page can usefully follow the Contents list, and you will almost certainly get credit for including such a page, even though your lecturer may do no more than glance at it.

Point 5 is particularly important in student writing. There is a strong temptation to include comments about how you felt, or to give a date for every stage of your working, or to identify the exact laboratory you used. This isn't appropriate. You are writing about your project, not about your own life and work, and you must concentrate on the subject matter itself.

Some examples of what can happen will clarify this; they all come from one set of student reports which I recently marked, but they are only too common in much student writing:

> The best part was using Autocad, as I'd not used it before ...
> The write up in the lab book is going well ...
> On Thursday 13 May, we concluded that it was time to move on to the manufacturing stage, and we divided the work equally ...
> I feel that a bit more time should have been allocated to this stage ...

None of these extracts increases my knowledge of the project itself: they are all about the writers' experience, and this isn't relevant to the report.

Generally speaking, scientific and technical writing is impersonal, and in most cases reports will be written in a style which reflects this – *It is recommended that* rather than *I recommend*. Nevertheless, there may be occasions when the only sensible way to write is by using 'I', for instance in a visit report where you are showing your personal response to what you saw or did. This is unlikely to happen in your time as a student, and for practical purposes, assume that you will never write 'I' in any of your reports. When you have been taking part in a group project, it might be acceptable to use 'we', but you need to check this with your lecturer.

Much scientific and technical writing is longer than it needs to be, either because it hasn't been well structured and so material is repeated, or because the writing itself uses unnecessary words. It's important, of course, to include all the information which is required, but if it is to be written effectively, it must not be wrapped up in excess words. For instance, in the sentence:

> The components were constructed or machined in a number of different ways to the required design specification

the words 'in a number of different ways' add nothing to the reader's knowledge. If the methods are described, the reader gains extra information, but the fact that 'a number of different ways' were used is not helpful. The important message is:

> The components were constructed or machined to the required design specification.

Sometimes a wordy style is ugly, as the reader is taken over the same words without the thought being moved on. In a report on an experiment, a student wrote:

> A water bath was heated to 20°C. Another was heated to 40°C, and a third was heated to 60°C.

This rambling style involves the reader in too much repetition, without giving adequate help – how can these three water baths be identified in the future? It would have been much better to write:

> Three water baths, A, B and C, were heated to 20°C, 40°C, and 60°C respectively.

Two further points from the list above need further discussion: the use of diagrams, which follows, and the need to check, which will be analysed more fully in the section on dissertation writing (see page 89).

▶ Diagrams

Fortunately, diagrams can nowadays be prepared on the computer, and the effort of drawing them can generally be avoided. However, some decisions about diagrams still have to be made by the report writer, who is just as responsible for the quality of the diagrams as for the quality of the words – and also for their originality. The rules about plagiarism, and the law of copyright, apply as much to diagrams as to words, and if you take a diagram from someone else's work, you must make this clear, by giving the source of the diagram immediately beneath its presentation.

A diagram is intended to make a visual impact on the reader, clarifying and reinforcing the message of the text. In order to do this, the diagram itself must be clear. If it is asked to carry too much information, or the detail is reproduced in too small a scale, the visual impact is lost; if, for example, letters and numbers are too small for easy reading, they may be misread – 5, 6 and 8 look very similar if they are not clearly reproduced. This is especially important when the report is photocopied, and some clarity thereby lost.

Colour may also be lost in the photocopying, and in any case it should be used with discretion. Many male readers may be colour blind as far as red and green are concerned, and if these colours are used, for instance to distinguish lines on a graph, many readers will not be able to interpret the information in the diagram.

The writer is responsible for deciding in the first place that a diagram is needed, and how much detail it should show. He or she also has to decide where the diagram will appear: will it be within the text itself, or in an appendix at the end? The convenience of readers is the major deciding factor: does the reader need to see the diagram while reading the text, or is it supplementary only? Generally, long series of tabulated figures which won't fit easily onto a page, or detailed schematic diagrams, or computer flow charts, are better in appendices. Smaller diagrams, which illustrate the discussion in the text, should be available to the reader without the nuisance of turning over several pages and working in two areas of the report at the same time.

A diagram should never interrupt the flow of the text, by being placed in the middle of a sentence, or in a closely reasoned argument. The reader will expect the topic shown in the diagram to be introduced and then the diagram to be presented, followed by the discussion. The writer has to assess whether there is room on the page for this order to be maintained.

The diagram also needs to be clearly identified. It should have a figure number and a short title, usually placed immediately under the diagram itself. The number may simply be sequential, or, in the case of a longer report, it can consist of two pieces of information, the section number of the main section of the report in which it occurs (the subsection number is ignored), followed by a sequential number. Thus, Figure 3.4 is the fourth diagram found in the third section of the report.

Readers need to be told when the diagram is to be used. Within the text, a reference will make this clear, so that (see Figure 3.4) lets readers know that the diagram with this reference is of use at this point of the report. If they don't have this indication, they may either ignore the diagram or look at it out of the appropriate context.

The clear, unambiguous presentation of diagrams is important for the reader; so too is the presentation of the report as a whole.

▶ **Professional presentation**

A report is the product of a professional writer, and it should look professional. The reader will inevitably look at the document before starting to read it, and if the appearance is less appealing than it should be, the reader will start with a feeling of depression; you don't want the person who marks your work to feel like this before even looking at what you've written.

The title page of your report is the first part to meet the reader's gaze. It should contain the appropriate information (see above, page 65), presented in a sensible font, nothing fancy (Gothic print, for example, looks fussy and unprofessional) and a reasonable size (perhaps 14 point for the title itself). Don't add meaningless diagrams or colour to the title page, and especially don't be tempted by clip art, which is childish and not even original.

The main text of your report should be printed on one side of the paper only, in 12 point, using a simple font with serifs, such as Times New Roman. Leave adequate margins on all sides of the page, roughly 40mm on the left and not less than 25mm elsewhere. Don't indent paragraphs, but leave an extra line blank before you start a new paragraph. Always number the pages of your report, using one sequence of arabic numbers throughout, but excluding the title page.

Generally speaking, your title page will be followed by Acknowledgements, if there are any, on a page by themselves; the Contents will also be on a new page, and so will the Summary, whether you put it at the beginning or the end of the document. The Introduction – remember that if you're using a numbering system, this will be the first numbered section – will also begin on a new page. In a long report, you might choose to begin each major section on a separate page; it would not be appropriate in a short report.

At the end of the document, your Appendix or Appendices, each identified by a letter, will again start on a new page or new pages, and your references will occupy a page or pages by themselves. Check that all diagrams are in their correct places, and appropriately labelled.

You will need some kind of binding for your report. If it's a final project report, you may be given a standard binding, perhaps printed with the name of your department and institution. If not, choose a simple and inexpensive binding which you could reuse if necessary, for instance slide bar binding. Make sure that your margins are sufficiently wide, as few things irritate markers more than having to dismantle a report because the first words on each line are obscured by the binding. This is almost as bad as finding that each page is in its own plastic sleeve, so that it has to be taken out before it can be marked and then put back. These things may seem trivial to you, but to the lecturer who has fifty reports to mark, they become near-obsessions. Remember reader goodwill.

One critical stage of report preparation has been left out: checking. This isn't because it isn't important – it's essential – but it's covered in some detail at the end of the section on dissertations. If you have to write a final project report and not a dissertation, you need to turn now to page 89.

▶ Dissertation writing

Towards the end of your course, you may be required to write a dissertation, to be assessed as part of your final degree or grade. This has much in common with report writing, and I shall often refer you to an earlier part of this chapter, but it has also some distinctive features which need to be discussed. As before, it's essential that you acquire any regulations or guidelines provided by your department, and adhere to them at all times. This section gives general advice and support only.

Choice of subject

The topic you choose for your dissertation obviously depends on your subject, and on the aspects which have especially interested you. Think back over courses which seemed particularly attractive, for which you regularly got good marks, or for which you read extra material with interest and pleasure. This is important: you will spend a great deal of time with your dissertation subject, gathering information, organising and writing it, and if it doesn't appeal to you, or you get bored with it, you will have a hard time producing an impressive dissertation.

It isn't a choice for you alone. One or more of your lecturers will probably be in charge of organising dissertations, and will give you general advice; when you have some idea of the area in which you would like to work, you will have a supervisor with expertise in your chosen field, who will guide you through the whole process of preparing your dissertation, and who will be available to help you if you run into difficulties.

A dissertation timetable

You may need help as you begin your work to try to form some kind of timetable for preparing your dissertation. You will be given a final date by which it must be submitted; before that, you need time for checking, correcting errors and rechecking (see page 89); at the beginning, you need to establish a date by which you will have written your objectives, prepared a chapter by chapter synopsis and discussed it with your supervisor; in the middle of the work, you need points at which experiments must be concluded, field studies carried out, interviews completed, and so on. Try to make yourself as realistic a timetable for all this as you can, with help where appropriate; you probably won't keep to it, but at least you can recognise when you are falling behind, and can readjust your programme. Always leave yourself extra spaces, gaps in which you can concentrate on other work, revise for exams, or just take a break from the stress of your academic work.

Narrowing down the subject

Almost inevitably, at an early stage you will make the mistake of trying to cover too large a subject. It's an easy error: you feel that if you choose a very small, specific area, you might not find enough information. This is highly unlikely. Generally speaking, the smaller and more precise your choice of subject, the easier it will be to produce something really interesting, perhaps even original. You may not be able to make such decisions straightaway: you may need to start with a wider topic and narrow it down as you talk to people about it and start to look at the literature available.

The library or libraries at your disposal now play an important part in your preparation. You aren't asked at this stage to add to the sum of human knowledge; that will come later if you decide to write a PhD thesis – which is beyond the scope of this book. You do, however, need to find out what other people have said about your possible topic, and, if you can, to see a theme or a synthesis of ideas which hasn't been handled in quite this way before. If your subject is developing rapidly, you may need to look for very up-to-date material, using articles in journals, conference proceedings or Internet sources rather than published books.

You will probably have to provide your supervisor with draft material: a provisional title, an indication of your objectives, a note of some of the main sources of your reading, a synopsis, and some idea of the methodology you wish to employ. Any of this may change, and it's wise to discuss your ideas at an early stage – your supervisor will almost certainly make helpful comments about your ideas, but he or she has to have some basic material to work on. You may well find that your reading is the best place to start; read critically, and make sure that you make a note of everything you read – you will need to be able to look at it again at a later stage of your work, and of course you will need the reference for your literature survey section.

Identifying objectives

You are trying to establish sensible objectives for your dissertation, and just deciding on a narrow topic which interests you, useful though it is, isn't enough. You can't afford to be simply descriptive; you have to show your skills of selectivity, analysis and synthesis. To do this, you need to have a focus, often in the form of questions to which you are going to find answers.

This can be a good way of identifying your objectives: why does something happen, how generally does it happen, are there exceptions, what would happen if ... ? The answers to these questions will become clear (if they don't, that in itself might be an interesting subject) as you study the subject further, but asking the questions helps to focus your thinking and gives you the basis for a dissertation structure.

In some subjects, the work will be largely experimental. In this case, you can identify your objectives in terms of a hypothesis or hypotheses which you are going to test; this will have the same effect of focusing your ideas.

When you feel that you are beginning to clarify your objectives, write them down. This is not just because your supervisor will want to see them, but because the very act of writing will help to crystallise your ideas. You may amend your objectives later, but you have a basis for your work.

▶ Organising the material

As with a report, a dissertation needs a logical structure, and in exactly the same way, you need to organise your thoughts before even thinking about the writing stage. You are likely to need a series of chapters, and each chapter may have subsections, again, as in a report. You are unlikely to be given any headings in the case of a dissertation, as so much will depend on your subject, but you already know that you will have to write:

- an Abstract (to be written last)
- an Introduction
- a Literature Review
- chapters on experimental work and results, or Theorem and Proof, or investigations and their results – the evidence you are working on
- an important Conclusions chapter in which you bring together the threads of your evidence and assess them, or show how far you have been able to prove, disprove or amend your original hypothesis
- probably a Further Work or Recommendations chapter, in which you show possible applications or further developments
- references to work that you have quoted or referred to directly.

These sections, vague as they are, give you a framework, and as you read on and clarify your objectives, you will start to see other chapter headings, or possible sections within your chapters. Your aim is to lead the reader through your work in a series of logical steps, leading to your conclusions. Use a spider diagram for each chapter (see pages 34–6 and 71–3), to help you to sort out your ideas, to group them, and to find a suitable logical order.

You will know from the information you have been given how long your dissertation should be. Generally, an undergraduate dissertation is between 10 000 and 15 000 words in length, and a Master's degree dissertation between 15 000 and 20 000 words. Other qualifications have their own regulations about length. Nobody will count the number of words in your writing, but examiners have an instinct born of long experience about such things, and it isn't wise to risk being far off the mark, as you may be penalised if you are outside the acceptable limits.

Word allocation

As soon as you are reasonably happy with the outline plan of your dissertation, check the number of words you are allowed, and, very approximately, allocate an appropriate number to each chapter or major section. Deal in hundreds of words – you can't hope to be exact. If you can, ask your supervisor to comment on your word allocation – it's always useful to have a second opinion. (An average page of type, double spaced and 11 point, has about 350 words in it.)

This is a very important step. As you write up your dissertation, you will be keeping the word allocation in mind. Of course, it will often turn out to be wrong – you couldn't know for sure at the beginning how much information you would have at each stage of the writing. But it allows you to ask questions, and that is its great benefit.

If you used far more words than you expected in a particular chapter, ask yourself:

- Have I included irrelevant material?
- Have I gone into too much detail at times?
- Am I repeating material unnecessarily?
- Is my style wordy and rambling?

If you honestly answer 'no' to each of these questions, then ask:

- Am I totally justified in using so many words in this chapter, was my original estimate wrong, and where do I save words in order to accommodate all these?

If you used far fewer words than you expected, ask yourself:

- Have I left out something important?
- Have I treated some aspect of the work superficially?
- Have I justified all that I've said, with closely reasoned argument and supporting evidence?
- Am I using too few words, and not explaining the process/ evidence/experiments sufficiently?
- Are all my sentences grammatical, or am I tending to write in note form?

If you honestly answer 'no' to each of these questions, then ask:

- Am I totally justified in using so few words in this chapter, was my original estimate wrong, and where can I use the extra words at my disposal most effectively?

When you start writing, you will probably feel very nervous. It can feel very final (although of course it isn't) to commit words to PC. Don't feel that you have to start at the beginning. Choose a comparatively easy section, however short, and write that first. There is a great psychological hurdle to be overcome in starting, and you will feel very much more positive and optimistic once you have written something. You may also want to draft-write at least some parts of your dissertation, and to discuss them with your supervisor. Check at what points it's acceptable for you to do this.

While much of the structure of a dissertation follows that of a report, there are some differences which you need to know about, especially in the Introduction and Literature Review, and these will be discussed in turn below.

The *Introduction* of a dissertation is very similar to its equivalent in a report. It will probably be short, but it will set out your objectives, or the hypothesis you are going to question, and will state briefly why this is of interest to readers, and/or why the ideas in the dissertation are important. You will also need to explain your methodology; you may, if it seems appropriate, give a brief synopsis of each chapter.

A *Literature Review* has three main aims:

- it demonstrates your awareness of the main writing and current state of thinking in your chosen area
- it highlights the limitations of current knowledge, or gaps in that knowledge
- it shows how work already published relates to your chosen topic.

As you read round your topic, you must note all published material that is relevant – don't risk having inadequate information later. It's useful to keep a card index of all the material you use, books, articles, computer resources and so on, and to note not only the details you will need for your references, but also what the coverage is, the author's point of view, any particular method adopted within your source.

You are not simply going to record all the material you have used. You have to evaluate it. This means that you must consider whether the author represents a particular school of thought on the subject, and whether he or she has dealt with it in a fair and unbiased way; whether the methods used are justified, and whether they are at variance with methods used by other authors; whether they represent new thinking, perhaps contradicting established thought; whether there are gaps in the coverage of the topic, which perhaps you can exploit.

This process of finding, reading and assessing the literature of your topic is time consuming (make sure that you allow enough time in your planning), but it helps you to establish where you stand, why you want to work on a particular topic, and how your work fits into the scholarship of your subject as a whole.

Generally, your literature review will start with the more general books, and so on, on the topic, and then look in more detail at the main schools of thought, perhaps ending with any newly promulgated ideas.

How long your Literature Review should be is a matter for discussion with your supervisor. Again, it will depend on your subject: if the dissertation depends heavily on your own experimental work, you may have a short Review; if you are following in a long tradition of research in the topic, you may have very many references to give. In either case, check that you have all the relevant details, and that you give them in a clear and consistent form throughout this chapter of your dissertation.

▶ Appropriate style

The style of a dissertation is as formal as that of a report, and the twelve points which formed a checklist of style earlier (see page 75) apply to dissertations as well. As you have a less rigid format in a dissertation, it's easier to ramble or to include irrelevant detail about your own reactions to the work you've done: be aware of the danger, and avoid it.

You will be using a wide range of sources in your writing, and some you will quote from or refer to directly. Take great care to give all the appropriate bibliographical details, using the Harvard system (see page 31) unless you are told differently. Of all your writing, this is perhaps the occasion when you are in the greatest danger of using someone else's work accidentally; your supervisor or your external examiner will almost certainly notice what you have done, and the penalties are severe. Keep all your working material, notes, logbook or whatever, so that if the worst happens and you do make such a mistake (deliberate plagiarism deserves a harsh response), you can at least produce this material as evidence of the work you carried out and perhaps of how the error occurred. You may also need this material to refer to if you have a viva (see page 150).

Inevitably, you will use a number of conventional forms in your writing, and you must follow what is laid down by your subject or your department. However, if you are not told otherwise, there are some guidelines which may be helpful.

Dates
Write dates out in an unambiguous and modern style, for instance as 5 March 1999, with no punctuation. Don't abbreviate the names of

months in the text, but if you need to do so in a table, for instance, then it is acceptable to write 'Sept.' 'Oct.' and so on. June and July are always fully spelt out. The year should be written out in full (1999 rather than 99), and if necessary clarified (the fiscal year, the academic year, and so on).

Numbers

As a general rule, only whole numbers under and including ten are written out as words, unless they are attached to a unit of quantity, such as 3mm or 10ml, or refer to sums of money, or where the context would make the rule difficult to apply, for example, 'the life of the system is between 8 and 12 years'. Round numbers are always written as words ('about a thousand people were present'). Inclusive numbers should include the fewest possible figures, for example 134–5, 1697–9, although in writing 'teen' figures, it is usual to repeat the 1, as in 1914–18.

A number at the start of a sentence should always be written as a word; if this causes a problem, reorder the sentence.

If you are writing a mathematical dissertation, you will have other decisions to make, for instance about how theorems are to be displayed and numbered. Follow the practice of your department.

Units

Appropriate units should be used. SI abbreviations are the same in the plural as in the singular, for example 1 m, 3 m. (Note that the abbreviation m is used for metre or metres, not for mile, miles or millions.)

Abbreviations

Many of the abbreviations which you use are closely associated with your area of work, and it's important to follow the conventions or to make the appropriate decisions, for instance whether to use °C or °K for temperature.

More general abbreviations have their own rules. Acronyms, that is, abbreviations which form words and which are usually spoken of in the abbreviated way, do not take full stops, as in UNICEF or MAFF. This applies also to the names of countries (UK, USA), and commonly nowadays to other initial letter abbreviations, such as DNA.

Abbreviations with a final letter which is the same as that of the full word have no final stop, as in St (street), Dr (Doctor); if the last letter is different, the full stop remains, as in Reg. (Regulation), no. (number).

If you quote organisational abbreviations, for instance in the name of a company, always check that you are using the correct form.

▶ Abstracts

The final sections of your dissertation to be written will probably be the Contents list, the Abstract (even though it goes at the start of the final document) and the Acknowledgements. The first of these follows the pattern given earlier (see page 83), and should present little difficulty; the second may be the hardest part of all to write.

You will have been given a length for your abstract, generally about 300 words. As you write the rest of your material, bear in mind that you will have to produce a very brief summary of the dissertation as a whole, and note any aspects which seem to you to be so decisive that they must be drawn to the reader's attention at the start. You are also providing source material for other people, that is, a guide to the coverage of your particular work.

Reports often contain a Summary of the most important aspects of the document, especially the Conclusions and Recommendations, and occasionally also an Abstract, which is a guide to the subject coverage for potential readers; in academic institutions this distinction tends to be blurred. The name Abstract is usually given, which is a précis of the dissertation, including the conclusions you have drawn, for instance about the hypothesis you chose to work on at the beginning.

Your first draft of the Abstract should be too long. It's much easier to cut it back than to decide what else to include, so aim for an Abstract which is 400–600 words long. Next, check what can be cut out, and also whether you have used unnecessary words or repetition, or included too much detail. You should be able to work on your material until you get it to the right length – don't go over the number of words given; if the result is a few words short of that total, it probably doesn't matter.

Finally, you will write your Acknowledgements. Don't go over the top, thanking everyone you know who has ever given you help and support, and avoid humour. Concentrate on thanking your supervisor and any other staff who have been particularly helpful, and any outside sources of information that it's appropriate to acknowledge. If you have any doubt, always check whether they want to be acknowledged: sometimes organisations which have given you specific information, for instance about financial matters, may not want to be acknowledged. If you feel awkward about this, just thank them in general terms without giving the name – much as I have to do when quoting examples of poor writing!

Your dissertation is now almost ready, but before you present it, there's one most important stage left – checking.

▶ Revision and checking

Revision is less a stage than a continual process as you prepare your material. Every time you talk to your supervisor, you may have to revise some aspect of what you are preparing. Further reading or discussions may affect your conclusions; the work itself may lead you to revise some aspects of your writing. Be flexible enough to do this, even though it seems to be a great nuisance at the time. You don't want to realise at your viva that there were ideas that you should have taken note of, but didn't.

Checking is much more of a last effort, but so important that you must leave time for it. Nowadays most students write their dissertations straight onto the computer; this saves time and allows you to move material round as you see fit, but it also presents a problem. We are all the very worst people to check our own writing. We know what we wanted to say, and so that's what we read, even if in fact we've written something else.

The first level of checking is to use the computer spellcheck (making sure that it uses English rather than American forms), and to read what's on the screen. This will draw your attention to some typing or spelling errors, but not, of course, to those which make a different word: these may be words which are similar in form but used differently, such as *principle/principal*; they may be words which sound the same, such as *site/sight*; they may result in nasty grammatical errors, such as a *their/there* confusion. None of these will be found by your computer, and they are very difficult to see from a reading of the screen. The most notorious of these confusions is *not/now*, which reverses the meaning, as in 'This point of view is now discredited'/'This point of view is not discredited'.

The next level of checking is from a printout. This has advantages: it's a more normal way of reading than from a screen, and you can see a much wider area of your work, comparing several pages at once if you need to do so. If you can, leave your work alone for 48 hours and then read it again – you are much more likely to notice mistakes than if you read it straightaway.

Check each section of your writing in this way, and make a note of decisions you have made; these may in themselves be unimportant, such as whether you spell organise with an s or a z, but you need to be consistent. Check also that you are using abbreviations or symbols, and capital letters, in a consistent way, and again note your decisions, as otherwise you won't remember them.

You may want to ask a friend or colleague to read your dissertation. If you can, persuade someone with little knowledge of the subject to read it for the expression, especially if you aren't writing in your first language; then, perhaps on an exchange basis, try to get someone who does know at least something about the subject to read it to see if there are any obvious errors or omissions.

All this takes time, and you need to allow for the checking stage in your preliminary planning. When you have corrected all the errors that have been pointed out to you, I'm sorry, but you need to check the whole thing again. It's surprising how often correcting one error creates another. When you have printed out or photocopied the correct number of copies of your dissertation, check that all the pages are there in the right order. Photocopiers can skip a page, and printers can jam. You have (of course) numbered your pages, so it shouldn't take long to complete this stage of checking.

Time runs out, and checking is a very boring task. It's worth remembering that examiners are only human, and if they see obvious errors as they start to read your dissertation, they will assume that you are a careless, unprofessional person, and that therefore your scientific or technical work will be slapdash, too. If this seems unfair, think of it like this: your future employers will react in exactly the same way.

▶ Key points

Reports
- ▶ Win the goodwill of your reader by giving your report a professional appearance, a clear structure and an accurate, concise writing style
- ▶ Choose an appropriate format and organise your material before you begin to write
- ▶ Follow the checklist on page 75 as you write your report
- ▶ Don't include chatty, personal comments in a scientific or technical report

► Use diagrams when they will help the reader; set them out and label them according to the conventions

► Make the right impact on the reader by using a suitable font, a clear layout and a sensible binding

Dissertations

► Choose your subject wisely after taking advice, and make yourself a dissertation timetable

► Identify your objectives, as this will help you to clarify your ideas

► Develop a framework for your dissertation and allocate words

► Record and evaluate all your reading

► Write in a formal style, following conventions in setting out numbers, dates, abbreviations and so on

► Revise your work regularly, and leave time to check it thoroughly at the end. If possible, ask someone else to read it too

Part Three
Speaking Skills

5 Speaking as Part of a Group

School work tends, even today, to be individual; industrial work is almost always carried out in groups. Further and higher education try to bridge this divide, and you will soon find that, while some of your assignments are to be completed by you as an individual, others are to be worked in pairs or small groups.

As scientific and technological knowledge develops at a tremendous rate, it becomes ever more important that people work in groups. No one person is likely to have a sufficient range of expertise to research or develop a product or system single-handedly, and from the first stages of training in a company, employees will be expected to operate as part of a team. Indeed, students at job interviews often forget to mention that part of their experience is working in groups to achieve a common aim: it is likely to be an aspect on which the interviewers place considerable emphasis (see page 183).

In this chapter, I look at group work in the context in which many students meet it early in their courses, that of the group presentation. Nevertheless, many of the points made will apply to any group or team, working on any aspect of the subject.

► Group members

Members of the group may be brought together in either of two ways: they may be put into a team by the member of staff responsible for the project, or they may choose to work together because they are already friends. Either way, there is unlikely to be any real consideration of their range of abilities or personalities, at least at first, when nobody knows anybody else very well. This can be a difficulty, as ideally the team might have an obvious driving force, someone else with graphic skills, a member with leanings towards meticulous administration and co-ordination, and so on. In a company setting, the distribution of abilities might be better known and taken into account; in education, particularly early on in a course, this is difficult.

Nevertheless, there are some considerations worth bearing in mind. If the class includes a small number of mature students with practical industrial experience, they may well choose very quickly to work together, when it would be more helpful for younger students if they joined different groups and so spread their expertise around the class. A similar pattern may be followed by overseas students with the same first language – it is understandable that they should want to work together, but it will not help them to integrate with the rest of the class or to develop their skill with the English language if they remain as a group. They may also be deprived of help if the lecturer is unfamiliar with their language and so fails to notice technical mistakes or inadequacies early enough to put things right.

However the group is formed, it undertakes certain responsibilities, of which the first is that it should become a team, each member helping and supporting the others. They do not have to become friends. There may indeed be problems with a group in which two people are already friendly, while the third is unknown or even disliked – this third person may be left out of discussions, information may not be passed on and, later, he or she may even be left out of rehearsals for the presentation, so that the weak link becomes apparent at the event. Within a company, people have to work together whether they like one another or not, and the same is true of group work in education. At the same time, a genuine and serious personality clash may come to the attention of the lecturer in charge, and a change may then be made – as it would be in a company if work was hampered by disagreement. It is worth commenting that such a solution would do little to enhance the career prospects of those concerned.

▶ Co-ordinating the group

A group needs someone to act as co-ordinator. I've deliberately avoided the word 'leader', which suggests someone making decisions and ordering their implementation; such authoritarianism will soon produce resentment among the others. It is better to have a key member who is able to put group decisions into words so that they can be finalised, who will suggest further discussion or the need to make a decision, who can get a sense of what everybody wants. It is essential to choose this person wisely, not just to accept an immediate volunteer – putting off the decision until the group has had the chance to talk together for a little while may result in the wiser choice of someone who is willing to listen, speak little, but show a thoughtful assessment of the situation.

It is also important that nobody should feel left out of the group. This can happen as a result not just of unpleasantness but of good intentions – not asking a very shy person to speak in discussion, or 'speaking for' an individual whose command of the language is less good than that of the others. The co-ordinator should watch out for any sign that this is happening, but each member of the group has a certain responsibility towards the others.

In much the same way, no individual within the group must be allowed to 'take over'. There have been cases in which one or two strong personalities have insisted on choosing a topic in which they had an interest, but about which the others knew nothing; the information then 'belonged' to those who provided it, they therefore took charge of the actual presentation, and eventually the other members of the group opted out, ceasing to come to team meetings or rehearsals, and in effect preventing a proper group presentation taking place.

In a company, a group presentation is just that – the conveying of complex information by a number of people with a range of expertise but a common purpose. If the presentation is to potential clients and a contract is at stake, that common purpose is all-important. No one person can be permitted to shine at the expense of the others, since the decision will be made on the basis of the group – 'do we want this team to work with us?' If they are clearly not able to work together as a team, the answer must be 'no'.

For the purposes of this chapter, I will assume that you are working in small groups of three or four. The most important activity at the first meeting is simply getting to know one another, creating as far as possible a pleasant working relationship, and becoming aware of any particular expertise. It is useful to ask open questions, that is, those which encourage people to talk rather than just say yes or no. 'How are you finding the course?', 'What sort of accommodation have you found? Who are you sharing it with?', 'How do you feel about the idea of talking to an audience?' are likely to generate conversation. The last of these questions may also produce a useful answer, such as 'I've done it several times before, and it isn't so bad', or 'I hate the talking, but I quite enjoy making visual aids as long as I can get to a computer' – useful clues for the future.

It's unlikely that major decisions will be made quickly at this stage, but one activity is important – the group needs to exchange telephone numbers, e-mail addresses or any other means of staying in contact with one another. Apart from the obvious need, this will also help to bind the team together, making each feel that he or she has something to offer the others.

▶ Choosing the topic

Before long, you will need to consider the topic on which your group has to work, and to ask whether anyone has particular knowledge or contacts which might be useful. Sometimes the topic has been given by the lecturer, and no change is allowed; at least this removes an area of possible disagreement. The group may be given a totally free choice of subject, but this is unlikely at an early stage of the course. More common is for the team to have a limited choice of general topics, within which they can choose the specific area in which they want to work. If this is so, there are two essential requirements: as a group, you must agree about the choice, and the topic must be narrowed down to the limits of what can sensibly be said in, for example, twenty minutes.

Members of the team will have different ideas about which subject should be tackled, but it is important that nobody tries to hijack the decision. A vote is a last resort and not recommended: it achieves a decision, but tends to leave those who voted against feeling resentful and perhaps left out of subsequent discussion. Look at possible topics and consider:

> Which subjects seem most attractive to team members?
> Does the team have any particular expertise or experience?
> Does anyone in the team have a useful contact, perhaps a family member in the industry?
> How much work will the subject entail? Will there inevitably be financial considerations, for example, and are the team members happy with this?
> Can members of the team already see how the subject could be approached in an interesting way?

Such discussion will probably reduce the possibilities to one or two topics, and the group should then be able to decide which they would like to work on; a 'second choice' may be sensible, in case an unforeseen difficulty makes the first choice less attractive, or several other groups have the same idea. Once a decision has been made, on the basis of sensible discussion, all members of the group should be prepared to give it their full backing, even if privately some would have preferred a different subject. As long as everyone has been able to contribute to the discussion, a group decision should be binding on the group.

Limiting your topic

The topic that your group finally chooses will almost certainly have to be narrowed down to something which can reasonably be handled in, say, twenty minutes. It is often difficult for an inexperienced team to recognise this, but it is generally true that the smaller the topic, the better the presentation. You will not be expected to come up with original research, but if your topic is too wide, you will end up generalising in a way which adds nothing to what the audience – basically the rest of your class – already knows; they will easily be bored. If, on the other hand, you choose a very small aspect of the subject, you may be able to describe an idea of your own, or suggest a possibility which your audience hasn't thought of before, and they will listen with interest. The level of knowledge which you are assuming on the part of the audience is that of your peer group, and so it will be much the same as yours to begin with. (Staff and research students may be invited to be part of your audience, and sometimes local industrialists may be invited, but they will not expect that you can tell them anything they don't already know at this stage of your course; it wouldn't be fair.)

In order to show this process of narrowing down the topic in more detail, I will use an example which was chosen in a construction management department, on the basis of a subject popular among students in their first year of study.

One among the short list of topics given to the class by the lecturer was 'Energy saving within the university'. A group choosing to present for twenty minutes on this subject would at once realise that as it stands, it might be the subject of a whole book. What should they do? How can they narrow it down? The process might be something like this:

Stage 1
'Energy' is a huge topic, with lots of different aspects. Suppose we choose one? Which? Heating and lighting are the obvious ones. There's a problem with choosing heating – buildings are controlled centrally, and we'd have to talk to the engineers who control it. We'd also probably be talking about huge sums of money, and it's all a bit out of our experience.

So what about lighting? We could choose a particular aspect of lighting, and it would be fairly easy to show what we meant.

Right, we'll look at lighting rather than other forms of energy, but we must remember to make that clear to the audience at the beginning of our talk, so that we don't get asked questions about heating!

Stage 2
The topic says 'the university'. That means the whole campus, indoors and out of doors. That's an idea, we could look at outdoor lighting; don't suppose anyone else would think of that. The lighting isn't always very good; some of us don't like taking particular paths at night. That's a possibility.

On the other hand, we could look at indoor lighting in a particular building, one we all know. If the audience knows the building as well, they will be able to relate easily to what we're saying. What about this building, in which our department is situated? Everybody knows that. Good.

Stage 3
We've now got two possibilities, outdoor lighting on the campus, and the lighting of this building. Some of it's very good – we've noticed that the computer rooms are really well lit. Perhaps it would be easier to choose somewhere that isn't well lit, so that we could make suggestions for saving energy and improving the lighting – it would give us a positive message. The corridors aren't too good, especially the top floor. My tutor's muttered about inadequate lighting in his room. Come to that, the lecture room we have our class in is a bit odd – the natural light seems to be in the wrong place and there are always lights left on when we get there.

Stage 4
We've narrowed it down to lighting, and to three possible areas for energy saving: the top corridor, your tutor's room, and this room we're in. We can forget the tutor's room, as only people who are his tutees will know it, and that will cut out a lot of the audience. What about the corridor? We'd really need to redesign it, make it wider, redesign the building – not very sensible, perhaps. What could we do about this room?

Stage 5
We've already said that the natural lighting doesn't seem to be helpful, but perhaps we're using the room the wrong way round. Would moving the chairs round make a difference? Perhaps we could try it. And lights are always left on. Why? What about daylight sensors, which would control the lights automatically? We could find a manufacturer and send for some information. It would also help if the light switches weren't so scattered that you have to walk all round the room to switch them off. Perhaps even notices asking people to switch off the light if they're the last to leave the room, and that would cost next to nothing.

Stage 6
We've obviously got lots of good ideas about the room, some we can try for ourselves and some we could ask about. We'll have plenty to say. Everybody knows the room, too, so they'll see the point of our suggestions. Right, can anyone see any problems with that, or are we all happy?

So a huge topic, energy saving within the university, ends up as improving the lighting in one lecture room – obviously a relevant aspect of the original subject, but small enough to be handled in twenty minutes, and familiar to the whole audience; this last is often a useful pointer in choosing what to say. The other ideas, which were perfectly sensible, were not dismissed out of hand, which might have upset the people making the suggestions, but were kept in mind until it was obvious that another topic had more possibilities.

Once the topic has been chosen and narrowed down, the work can be allocated between you. Again, it is important that everybody takes some responsibility; some tasks can be done most easily by one person, while others may take more than one. In the case of our example group, one person might take responsibility for writing to the manufacturer (or telephoning), while the whole group might meet in the room one evening and, having alerted the porter or security office, try moving the furniture round to see whether the current arrangement could be improved.

► Interviews

If interviews are needed, they should be handled with tact and an awareness that the time of a busy person is being taken. A phone call explaining what is wanted and requesting an interview is the first courtesy, and a time should be agreed. Students have on the whole clearly defined times when they can be available, and it's a good idea for the group to discuss this before making the call, so that they have a few possibilities ready. How many people should go to the interview is another question to be decided in advance. Everybody can help in deciding the questions to be asked, but it is often easier if only two people go – a large group gets in the way and tends to be less well focused than two well-prepared visitors.

If the interview is on company premises, it would be as well to confirm what has been agreed in writing, perhaps by e-mail (not least so that if the employee who has agreed to the interview is away ill, somebody else knows what is happening). A length of time will have been discussed, and good time-keeping is a matter of courtesy: if the interview is between 11 and 11.30, the group should be there a few minutes before 11, and should at least offer to go at 11.30. Such consideration will be appreciated – it might result in an extension of the time available, and it might be remembered later if any of the group applies for a vacation job. For the same reason, a brief letter of thanks should always be sent after the visit. Any company rules must be observed, and of course a camera must never be taken onto company premises without prior permission. However, companies are sometimes willing to lend slides or display material which could be used in a presentation, and it is worth asking if this is possible. One other comment about such visits: take notes. I heard a remark by someone whose company had taken a great deal of trouble to help a student group: 'They were nice young people and seemed bright, but they were here for the whole afternoon and didn't write a single word. We couldn't believe it – how did they expect to remember?'

The information is collected, and there will come a point at which the group's attention will shift to the preparation for the presentation itself. The lecturer will probably guide students as to how the preparation time should be allocated, but it would be unwise to be still gathering information up to the last week. There is much more to be done.

▶ Structure and team organisation

The group may need to decide how many are going to speak. For a twenty-minute presentation, two or three would be sensible, but if none of you has presented before, it would usually be acceptable for everyone to be included so that you all get some practice. However, you will first need to decide on an outline structure for the talk.

In a group presentation, there are always two parallel structures – the overall format, and the shape of the individual contribution. The team will need to consider the general format quite early in the preparation process. If we again take our energy saving group as an example, we can see that they might structure their presentation like this:

Stage 1
We've got to start with some introductions – the audience will need to know who we are and what we're talking about – and we must remember

to make it clear that our topic is limited to the lighting of the one room. If we've got someone in our group who's spoken in public before and has a good clear voice, perhaps that would be the best person to start us off.

Stage 2
Everyone knows the room, but perhaps they haven't all thought about the lighting, so we'd better explain what the current problems are. If we're giving our presentation in the room we're discussing, then the room itself will be a sort of visual aid, and we can ask the audience to look round and see what we mean; that will also help to make them feel involved in the presentation.

Stage 3
We've got various suggestions for improvement, and they seem to fall into two categories: small things like the notice, which we can do ourselves, and bigger changes such as sensors, for which we're dependent on the manufacturer's help. Which type shall we handle first? Perhaps we could start with the smaller changes – that won't take much time, but it will get us going with practical recommendations – and we can make the point that we've tried moving the chairs and tables round for ourselves.

Stage 4
Now we can get a bit more technical, which will please the staff in the audience, but we mustn't overdo it, as it's still a presentation not a report. We can outline how sensors will work, and look at how feasible they are. There are some sensors already in the library, so perhaps we could ask one of the staff if there are any problems. What about moving the light switches? That might go into the same section.

Stage 5
Could we include a sketch of what the room might be like if all these changes are made? Visual aid? We'll have to think about that. Cost? That's going to be very important, and so someone is going to have to give an estimate of what each change will cost. Can we look at a possible payback period? We ought to have some idea about that, even if we don't actually use it in the presentation – someone might ask.

Stage 6
Let's be realistic! The university isn't going to spend the earth getting hi-tech lighting in one lecture room, so let's review our ideas in the light of what they might spend – putting up a notice about switching lights off would cost virtually nothing, so that can certainly be included! So we'll end with a summary of what can easily and cheaply be done, and a recommendation that the department considers our proposals as soon as possible. That should impress!

The presentation now has a sensible shape. Some changes can be made later, in the light of the information which the group finds out, but the general structure is realistic and helpful to the audience. We should perhaps look in more detail at some of the group's considerations.

Introductions

At the beginning of a presentation, the audience needs a certain amount of reassurance. Are they in the right place, how long will the presentation last, when can they ask questions? If answers aren't provided right at the start, the audience will go on wondering, and this will distract them from what is being said. Unless it is absolutely certain that every single person in the audience knows every speaker, the presentation must start with introductions, by the first speaker or by whoever is taking a chairing role.

As each individual is introduced, he or she should acknowledge the introduction – perhaps by a smile at the audience, or by saying 'good morning'. As the audience will also want to know who is talking about which aspect, the subject can be included, like this:

> We'd like to talk to you this morning about the problems of lighting ... and how energy can be saved ... I am Jane Thomas, and I'll start our presentation by pointing out some of the current problems, some of which you've probably already noticed ... Stephen Dale will then suggest some quick and easy solutions, followed by Sue James with some which are more technical. Lastly, Alastair Macpherson will cost our suggestions for you, and highlight those which, we're sure you will agree, should be implemented straightaway.

The audience already has a good deal of information about the subject, how it is to be tackled, the order in which the problems will be handled, and which speaker is responsible for each section. They will also want to be told that the presentation will last for twenty minutes, after which they can ask questions. Notice, too, how the audience has already been drawn into the presentation: they have been told that they are aware of some of the problems (a little flattery, 'we're all in this together'), the costing has been thought through for their benefit (don't underestimate the impact of 'for you'), and there are to be positive recommendations at the end which they are likely to approve of. Their attention has been captured, and they will want to listen.

This is a strong beginning, and if Jane then uses the room in which they are working and invites the audience to look round at each problem as she refers to it, they will start to feel that this is a talk prepared with them in mind, and therefore one which is worth concentrating on. Audiences tend to remember what is said at the beginning of a presentation, and so the opportunity shouldn't be wasted – if they are involved then, their attention is likely to be held for longer than if the first speaker sounds flat and uninterested (see also page 132).

▶ Technical content

The amount of technical detail included in the presentation is a difficult assessment. These are inexperienced students, and they won't be expected to present a great deal of technically complex material. Indeed, as we said earlier, there is a limit to what any audience can cope with just by listening. At the same time, the students are taking a technical course, and some of the lecturing staff may be in the audience. It would be foolish to give a whole talk on a superficial level, as if to members of the general public with no expertise in the subject. This is where our example group has to tread carefully. Some of its suggestions, such as putting up a notice, might come from anybody; it is still a perfectly sensible suggestion, but it doesn't involve any technical thought. Asking a manufacturer or two for details of sensors is a wise step: the group will be sent some technical information (especially if they made it clear in their request that they were going to speak to a technical audience), and if they can handle it competently, they are showing a more specialised interest, even if the level isn't very advanced. Similarly, they might try to find some technical detail from the library about the operation and effect of the sensors there.

There is always a danger that a group will acquire more technical material than it can handle, and will become confused in repeating it or fall prey to detailed questions from staff. Whatever technical information is used, it must be thoroughly understood by the whole team. This applies also to visual aids (see also page 124); sometimes a student group will reproduce a highly complex diagram on the screen, but find when they have to talk about it that it includes details which they not only don't need but which they don't understand. Anything which is told or shown to the audience is fair game for questions.

Realistic recommendations
It is a good idea for you to show, early in your course, that you have some appreciation of 'real-life' problems, especially those which have to do with money. If all the suggestions you offer are very expensive

and highly unlikely ever to be implemented, then they are not sensible suggestions, however technically feasible. Of course there is no harm in showing that you are aware that such possibilities exist, but always show that they are likely to be theoretical only, and that you have other more moderately priced recommendations to make as well. You may not be able to get exact costs for all your suggestions, but always have a rough idea – if you don't say, you will be asked.

Preparing for questions

Our group looked at the question of the payback period for their suggested improvements, as they recognised that, if they left this out of their presentation, someone would be likely to ask. This doesn't mean that they have to include the information, but that they must have some idea of the answer. There is a lot to be said for leaving out such detail, and then being able to say cheerfully to a questioner, 'Thank you. We thought someone might ask that, and so we've discussed it and we reckon ... '. This sounds very impressive.

An essential stage of preparing a presentation is always thinking about likely questions. The group should do this together, looking over all their material and asking 'When we've said all this, what are they likely to ask?' There are usually quite obvious areas for questions – cost, feasibility, maintenance, availability, safety implications, possible applications or further study – and no team should be caught out by not thinking of these things. If they have been unable to get the information, then at least they can say, 'We tried to find that, but nobody was able to give us what we wanted. We're sorry; perhaps someone in the audience could help?' This is a useful ploy when there are staff or research students present, and therefore a good chance that someone will have the missing information; if they haven't, then your inability to find out is seen as perfectly reasonable as nobody else knows, either.

When you have had a group session spent in thinking of likely questions, you might like to give a rehearsal of your presentation to a colleague outside the group, or to a mature student in the class, and ask if they can see any omission or probable question. This is an important stage in professional presentations for the same reason – nobody wants to be caught out by not knowing something which they really should have considered.

Conclusions

The final speaker in the group has a serious responsibility, that of concluding the presentation effectively. There is a terrible tendency for student – and other – presentations to peter out. This often takes the form of the last speaker ending with 'That's it', 'That's all we've got time for' or 'That's all we've got to say', even, alas, 'That wraps it up'. None of these is a very impressive ending! The audience will remember what is said at the end of the talk, and you want them to carry away a good, strong, useful message. Be positive. Repeat your most important recommendation, with a suggested action if possible, once more involving the audience, as in:

> We're sure that you will want to implement some of our less expensive suggestions, such as notices, straightaway; we hope others could perhaps be passed on to the Faculty for their consideration – and of course we'll be delighted to give them our findings in detail. Thank you all. We're sure there are questions you'd like to ask, and we're happy to answer them now.

Notice that 'we'll try to answer them' might be more accurate, but it sounds unsure and hesitant, when you want to leave the audience with an impression of knowledge and competence.

▶ Handling questions

The group has to prepare the answers to questions as far as possible; it must also discuss how the questions are to be handled. If more than one person tries to answer at the same time, or, worse, if one member of the group tries to answer all the questions without reference to the others, the audience gets no sense of a group working together as a team.

One person may be chosen to receive and co-ordinate all the questions; this helps the group to organise itself, gives a focal point for the questioners, and also gives a tiny but sometimes priceless amount of thinking time before an answer has to be given. The best person for this role is often the first speaker, chosen for speaking experience or abilities. In addition, if the first speaker is also the last, the presentation is rounded off; there is a sense of unity about it.

All questions are, then, addressed to the person who has this chairing role, and he or she may choose to answer – but not too often. The sense of the team effort must continue right to the end, and everyone, as far as possible, should take part in question time. On the whole, questions should be answered by the person who spoke about the specific aspect: the speaker who discussed costs will be the one to answer about costs. However, it is useful for speakers who have given an answer to finish by looking at colleagues and asking if they would like to add anything; if they don't, at least the opportunity has been given, and if the speaker hasn't perhaps given a very full answer, one of the other team members might be able to amplify it. Either way, it gives a good impression of the group acting together.

In the case of a difficult question, the person chairing the session has extra responsibilities. Often simply looking at the group members shows which one is ready to have a go, but if all are looking blank, it will be necessary to choose the most knowledgeable, or to try to answer without passing the question on to the group. If it's an impossible question in that nobody has any idea how to answer it, say so – above all, never bluff your way through. Someone in the audience will probably know the answer, and it will be embarrassing if they put you right. It's much more sensible to appeal to the audience for help, or to use the most common way out of the problem: 'I'm sorry, but I'm afraid we don't know the answer, but it's an interesting question and we'll try to find out and let you know.' If the group has worked hard at preparing the answers to likely questions, such a situation shouldn't arise too often.

▶ Group courtesy

We have stressed repeatedly that a group must be seen to be acting as a group; credit will be given for teamwork, but few things lose marks so quickly as clear signs that the group has fragmented, that it is four individuals making their own presentations rather than a team with a common purpose.

Once the topic has been chosen and structured by common consent, it has to be divided between the speakers. This is not a question of time. Too often, a group will think that as they have four members and a twenty-minute presentation, it stands to reason that each will speak for five minutes. If each then prepares five minutes, it will become clear at rehearsal that the presentation is too long – in this context, four fives equal about twenty-three. The time should never be divided in this way; it's the subject matter that is shared between the speakers, and the time is then allocated accordingly. In the case of our example group, the speaker with the technical part of the talk is likely to need more time than the others; the speaker who deals with the simple proposed changes will have less detail to give, and will therefore need less time.

There must be courteous agreement about this, and such decisions must be adhered to. It's disastrous if one speaker has been asked to speak for four minutes, and at the presentation he or she goes on for eight. Other members of the group are put into a very difficult position, and almost certainly the whole presentation will overrun. This is a major discourtesy by one speaker, both to the audience and to the rest of the team. The timing is decided, and then rehearsed, and if this is agreed and thoroughly practised, everyone should be able to keep to time with only a very small amount of latitude needed.

Timing can never be absolutely precise, and for this reason, you should always have a little bit of time in hand for emergencies. If you have been allocated twenty minutes, rehearse your presentation so that it takes seventeen. You then have three minutes for anything which is unforeseen, such as people arriving late and causing an interruption, or someone speaking a little more slowly than at rehearsal. Finishing a bit early is not a problem, as it simply allows more time for questions.

Courtesy will also show itself in the handovers between speakers. Each must be ready to introduce the next, indicating what aspect they will speak about – this reminds the audience, and also shows that the group members are at ease with each other. So when Sue James finishes her technical information for the audience, she will smile at them and say:

> Thank you. Now Alastair will discuss the costs of our proposals, and tell you our final assessment of the situation.

(The importance of smiling is discussed in more detail on page 140.) Alastair comes into position to speak, but starts by smiling at Sue and saying, 'Thank you, Sue.' He then picks up what she has just said: 'As you've just heard, I'm going to look at costs, but not just at costs – I'll be talking about what we see as the most cost-effective solutions.'

Cross-referencing within the presentation is another way of showing team courtesy: 'As you heard earlier from Jane ... ', 'I'd like to reinforce what Steve said earlier ... ' and so on. Above all, the team must have a common point of view. Any disagreement should have been resolved a long time ago; it should under no circumstances be allowed to show itself at the presentation. It isn't just words which give away to the audience that one of the group is unhappy about what is being said by another; body language (see page 142) such as a frown or slight shake of the head will also tell the onlookers what is happening.

If something does go wrong during the presentation, such as

someone forgetting what they were to say, a piece of demonstration equipment failing or a visual aid being shown at the wrong time, the team takes collective responsibility, and shows consideration and support – nobody sighs or frowns or mutters a cross word to a neighbour. If help has to be given, it should be given as quickly and unobtrusively as possible, but it is generally better to let the speaker sort out the problem rather than intervening, unless the situation is too serious and help is clearly needed.

Part of the courtesy demanded of a team is that each person listens with rapt attention to the other speakers. This is sensible, since if something is omitted by accident, or a point is made too early, it's as well for other speakers to know. It is also important for its effect on the audience. They are watching the whole team, not just the speaker, and if the others are clearly listening with interest, the audience feels encouraged to listen with interest, too. The opposite is also true. If the rest of the group is looking bored, or gazing out of the window, then the audience feels that what is being said is clearly not of any importance, and perhaps what is going on outside the window is better value for them, as well. If other speakers are sitting in full view of the audience and studying their notes, or exchanging a quick word, the audience will immediately be distracted, feeling that the presentation has obviously not been well prepared in advance.

▶ Group image

Listening attentively to each other helps to create your group image of efficiency and professionalism, part of which depends on your appearance, both as a group and individually. Talk about this in plenty of time, and look at the room in which you are going to present. Where will the speaker stand, so that the audience can all see and hear easily? Where will the people who are not speaking sit? They should certainly sit rather than stand, as it's very difficult to stand still and not to fidget. Chairs should be in place for them, in sight of the audience but well out of the speaker's way – speakers have been known to fall over their colleagues during a presentation.

Place the chairs at a slight angle to the audience rather than confronting them. The natural sight line of the group should be towards the speaker, and if they are sitting directly facing the audience, there is a temptation to stare at one person and then perhaps to want to laugh. The speakers should sit in the order in which they are going to speak, to help the audience in identifying them, and to make the changeovers as easy and quick as possible.

Presentations are formal occasions, and you will need to decide how you will address one another. The most common form of introduction nowadays, for both sexes, is first name and surname; after this, it is reasonable to use your colleagues' first names, as you would normally. Your style should be formal: it sounds strange if the first speaker starts with 'Good morning' and the second with 'Hello'. You will also need to think about how you will dress, bearing in mind what the tradition of your particular department is.

Student dress is usually very casual, and rightly so. You have little money for formal clothes, and you would like to be comfortable at work and in your leisure time. However, a presentation is formal, as we have said, and there are conventions about dress: for most such occasions, a business suit is appropriate for both men and women. This isn't as pompous as it may sound, since dressing appropriately for a presentation doesn't just help to give an impression of professionalism to the audience; it makes the speakers themselves feel more confident. Informal dress tends to make the wearer stand informally, and the opposite is also true: it is easier to carry oneself well and to have an air of self-respect if one knows one is dressed appropriately for the occasion. This applies also, of course, to job interviews.

The group should discuss this, and come to a sensible compromise. If only one speaker owns a suit, it might be as well to settle for light-coloured shirts, with ties for the men and dark trousers, and plain dark-coloured skirts or trousers for the women. This will give a general and acceptable air of professionalism.

▶ Rehearsals

We have deliberately stressed the idea that a group presentation demands group rehearsals. Inevitably, individual members of the team will take their own sections of the presentation and practise wherever they live; this is a good start, but it isn't enough. The group must rehearse together several times, preferably as early as possible while major changes are still feasible, and the night before, to make sure that everyone is ready. Partly, as we have said, this is a matter of timing. It isn't possible to time the presentation accurately without going through the whole event, putting all the sections together and allowing for the time taken by changeovers and the use of visual aids (see page 121). These always take longer than inexperienced speakers expect.

The visual aids themselves need to be checked, not just for accuracy but also for consistency within the group. Companies use logos and often a company style and colour in order to emphasise that the visual aids have been produced by the organisation rather than by individuals, and a student group can get something of the same effect by ensuring that the same colours are used for the same details, and that there is a 'team style': this is destroyed if one person uses hand-drawn visual aids while the others have all generated theirs on the computer.

Team members also need to be at ease with one another, and with what everyone is saying – there must be no last minute surprises. There is an additional reason for this: if one of the group is ill at the last minute and cannot take part in the presentation, the others must cover for the absentee, drawing as little attention as possible to the difficulty they face. If they can manage to give the presentation without anybody except themselves and the lecturer knowing that there is someone missing, they will have been very professional in their preparation and approach, and credit will be given for their achievement. Only thorough rehearsal as a team will make this possible. Illness or some other serious and unavoidable reason for absence can be a problem for any group working together, and if necessary the audience can be told briefly at the start – if, for instance, all the names are on the visual aids and it will be obvious that someone is absent; if the audience is put in the picture in this way, the problem should not be referred to again, and there should be no sense of the team making excuses for an inadequate performance. Needless to say, absence for a more trivial reason such as oversleeping is a very serious offence indeed, and will doubtless be regarded as such by staff marking the presentation.

By the time of the final rehearsal, the group will probably feel tense and a little excited by the challenge of making a presentation to their department. If they have worked well together, they can support and encourage each other, and generate a sense of enthusiasm. This is invaluable. I will say more in a later chapter about nerves (see page 133) and the importance of enthusiasm (see page 139), but team members who smile at one another and look confident as they move into position in front of an audience are halfway to being successful before they start.

▶ Key points

▶ If you are working together as a group, you will need a co-ordinator to help you to get to know one another, to make decisions and to organise the work

▶ Choose the topic for your presentation by sharing ideas, listening to one another and agreeing your choice. Co-operation is critical throughout the project

▶ Narrow down your subject until you can say something useful and interesting in a short time

▶ Decide on the structure of your presentation, and allocate time on that basis; each speaker needs to have a sensible amount of time, but all the contributions don't have to be of the same length

▶ Use the introduction to identify the speakers and the way in which you are going to handle your topic. Reassure the audience about the length of the presentation and when questions may be asked

▶ Make realistic recommendations and prepare for questions, co-ordinating your response

▶ Decide on the appropriate group image, discussing a common approach to dress, visual aids and style of delivery

▶ Rehearse until your timing is accurate and each of you is at ease with his or her contribution, and with other people's

6 Preparing Notes and Visual Aids

In Chapter 5, the first stages of preparation for a presentation were discussed in the context of speaking as part of a group. Individual preparation is similar, with the same emphasis on the need to narrow the subject down to manageable proportions, to identify the objectives and to plan the structure before attempting to look at the content in detail. Chapter 7 will give practical advice about the actual performance, such as using the voice and appropriate body language in order to build a rapport with the audience. In this chapter, I will look at a different stage of the presentation process: preparing and using notes and visual aids effectively. The comfort, and so the confidence, of the speaker will depend to a large extent on using prompts efficiently, while the response of the audience will be greatly affected by the quality of the visual aids.

Some speakers will be able to present without notes of any sort. Usually, such speakers have a high level of confidence based on years of experience of public speaking. If you are not in this category, you will probably feel better for having some kind of prompt just in case you forget what you are going to say or the order in which you were going to say it. There is absolutely no disgrace in using notes: many experienced and excellent speakers like to carry notes, even if they rarely refer to them.

There are, however, some ways of presenting information which are not recommended. Don't be tempted to learn the whole of your material by heart as if it were a part in a play. If you do this, your 'lines' will be inflexible, and any slight distraction may make you lose track of your speech; there is unlikely to be a prompter in the wings if this should happen. You may also feel that you don't want to look at the audience in case they provide a distraction; as a result, they may be left feeling that they are an irrelevance to your performance of your part.

▶ The dangers of reading

A much more common problem is faced by people who write out every word of their presentation on A4 sheets, and then inevitably read it. It takes considerable acting skill and experience to read to an audience without boring them; for most speakers, it is a highly dangerous thing to do. If you read, your eyes will be fixed on the words in front of you, so that eye contact becomes impossible – in the next chapter we shall discuss the importance of eye contact, but it's worth stressing now that if the audience is to listen to you and trust you, it's absolutely essential that you look at them.

There are other dangers in reading to an audience. We may read at 400 or more words a minute, while in a presentation we're speaking at about 110 words a minute. When we read our script, our eyes are constantly pushing us on to a greater speed, and our voice inevitably tries to follow suit; we get faster and faster, and the audience finds it increasingly difficult to hear or assimilate what we're saying. Again, you have an inflexible script, which becomes more important to you than the wellbeing of the audience. If you then take a quick glance at the audience, you risk losing your place, and if you are faced with an A4 sheet full of notes, it may take you a minute or two – which will feel to you like ten – to find the right words with which to continue.

A sheet of A4 paper is also large in comparison with a human face, and speakers are sometimes tempted to hide behind their notes; if they are very nervous and their hands shake, the papers may rustle in a very revealing way!

There is another, perhaps less obvious, hazard connected with reading from a full script. You sit down at your desk, with computer or pen, to write your notes. Your mind is at once put into writing mode, and the language which results is therefore written language – perfectly acceptable on the printed page, but slightly stiff and overformal if spoken to an audience. When we're talking to someone, we automatically adjust our language to speaking mode, less formal, more abbreviated and probably less grammatical – but perfectly comprehensible to the listener.

We can show the difference by using the information which we have just given in two forms: a formal written style first, and then an informal spoken style.

Written language

In making a presentation, there is an additional reason for avoiding a full written text: written English is very different from spoken English. If notes are written out in full, the writer, by the very fact of writing, will naturally use a formal style which is more appropriate to a document than to a presentation. The effect is unnatural, and alienates the audience.

If notes consist of key words and phrases only, the speaker has to create the sentence structure as he or she is talking; inevitably, the result will be the use of spoken rather than written language. The audience will feel that they are indeed being addressed by the speaker.

Spoken language

So when you're making a presentation, there's another reason for not writing everything out in full, word for word. In the English language, there's a big difference between the way we write and the way we speak. If we write everything out, then the very fact that we *are* writing locks us automatically into the written language, and then when we read it out loud, it sounds odd, like a book talking. It comes across as peculiar to the audience, unnatural and off-putting.

If we write out just the key words and phrases, we've got to *create* the sentences as we speak, and then just because we're speaking, we automatically use the *spoken* language and it sounds natural to people listening.

Analysis
Let's look at some of the differences between these two messages.

- The written form begins immediately with part of the message – 'In making a presentation ... '; it uses comparatively few words, and contains no abbreviations. The spoken version starts with a meaningless word. 'so', which simply helps to launch the speaker into the talk; it contains far more words, some of which are used only to help the flow of the sentence – 'then' is a frequent example. We also see the abbreviations which we use all the time in speech, such as 'you're' and 'we've'.

- There is much more repetition in the spoken language. Statements are repeated in different words, so that the audience has a second chance to hear them. An example of this is 'writing everything out in full, word for word'. When we are reading, we can take our time over the text, and so we don't need to have information given twice in this way.

- Words can in themselves be more or less formal. 'Alienates', 'inevitably' and 'indeed' are all more common in writing than in speech (although of course we may speak them under certain circumstances); 'big', 'odd' and 'off-putting' are words which we frequently speak, but would be much less likely to write. 'Just' is a spoken variant of 'only'.

- Punctuation and emphasis are also different. In writing, we can make use of quite complex and elegant forms of punctuation, such as colons and semi-colons. In speech, it's difficult to 'say' any punctuation apart from full stops and commas. We give emphasis by the tone of voice, but this can be shown in writing only by the clumsy device of using italics. If we want to emphasise effectively in writing, we have to do it by using extra words or by layout.

You will notice, incidentally, that the style I have adopted in this book is rather less formal than the example of formal writing which you've just looked at. I deliberately chose to write in a style which is a little closer to speech, in order to give the book a more friendly, immediate tone. If I were writing a scientific or technical report, for example, I would certainly choose a more formal style. As I said in Chapter 3, writing style must be adapted to readers and objectives.

Spoken style is adapted in the same way, although the differences may be less extreme. In casual conversation with friends, we use colloquialisms freely; if we share a local dialect, we may unconsciously strengthen it. When we attend a job interview, we will try to avoid slang and we may also lose something of our local accent, especially if the interview is away from our home area. We may be unaware of these changes; they are made unconsciously because we react instinctively to differences in audience and objectives.

A presentation is a formal occasion, although the exact level of formality will vary. Even so, people tend to talk less formally than in the past, and you will happily use contractions such as 'it's' or 'won't'; it also seems more acceptable in speech to use your own experience told in the first person than it does in writing. Even the formal language of the occasion is essentially spoken, rather than written, and must be so if the audience is to feel that you are talking to them rather than reading at them.

There are, then, dangers in either learning your script by heart or writing it out in full. Two forms of notes remain, both of which give a professional appearance and are comparatively easy to use: visual aids and note cards.

▶ Visual aids as notes

You will be preparing visual aids primarily for the benefit of the audience, but they can also be of great use to you as the speaker. If in your introduction you present a list of the aspects you will be discussing, you are reminded of the topics and their order, just by looking at the screen. If you show a list of key points, or build it up gradually with the aid of an data projector, it will act for you as a series of prompts. Illustrations which you are projecting can be used in the same way: you may show, for example, a block diagram of the circuit or a flow chart of the process that you are describing, and the diagram itself leads you from one point to the next in the correct order. It has become your notes for that part of the presentation.

On the whole, this is a professional and efficient way of using visual aids, but there is one danger: in an unconscious attempt to see the notes more easily, the speaker may gradually turn towards them, so that in time he or she is facing the screen and turning away from the audience. One way of overcoming the risk is to have an enlarged print-out of the information on the screen, placed on the table beside the projector or the computer. This must be sufficiently large to be seen from the speaker's usual position, that is, the speaker mustn't have to move forward to look down at the paper. If this is positioned carefully, there are now two ways of seeing it – by glancing either at the screen or at the sheet of paper in front of the speaker, that is, in either direction. If the image consists of a list of key points, then this can also be written on note cards, so that you can choose to look either at the screen or at the notes. Obviously if the illustration is in the form of a diagram, you will be using a pointer and therefore looking at the screen in order to point accurately, making eye contact with the audience when possible.

In using visual aids in this way, it's very important that you are at ease with what you are showing. This means plenty of rehearsal, so that there is no sense of surprise at what is on the screen, and no temptation to peer at it in order to see what to describe next. As with any form of notes, visual aids must not take up too much of your attention: it's the audience that matters most.

▶ Note cards

The most common form of notes used by professional presenters is small file cards. They have great advantages over A4 paper, in that they feel firm to hold, won't rustle even if your hands shake, and are small enough to be unobtrusive from the audience's point of view. They are also too small to contain much information, and so it's unlikely that you would lose your place and be unable to find it again quickly.

Nevertheless, in preparing your file cards it is as well to write on every other line and to leave plenty of space between the main points you are making; in addition, leave a wide margin at one edge of the card for your own notes, as described later. Look back at your organisation of the material, checking again the strong opening, logical progression of thought and effective ending. When you are happy with your structure, begin to make your notes, writing key words and phrases for each point, so that there are no complete sentences.

This form of note-writing helps to ensure that you will use spoken language in your presentation. As you look at each card, you will be reminded of the point to be made but you will have to form the words into sentences as you speak. Since you are speaking to the people in front of you, you will instinctively use a natural speech form rather than a formal written style. There is another advantage of using key words and phrases: as you rehearse, there is a slight risk that if you say exactly the same thing each time, you will start to hear yourself talking, and it can be distracting for a speaker if this happens. As you are forming your sentences afresh each time, the sense will be the same but the words slightly different, and the risk of listening to yourself is reduced.

The number of cards you use depends partly on the complexity of the information and partly on your own experience. You may choose at first to write out most of the detail; as you gain confidence through rehearsal, you may then be ready to rewrite your notes less fully; it is perfectly acceptable to use full notes (with the proviso of avoiding sentences) until you feel that you are ready to speak from less detailed prompts. As you finish with each card, simply move it to the back of the cards in your hand – throwing it down on the table, a common habit among inexperienced speakers, draws attention to your cards and may result in the audience counting them rather than concentrating on your message.

Content of cards

The main content of your cards will be your information, as described, but some material should always be written out, however well rehearsed and familiar it is. If you have to introduce colleagues, put their names on your cards, as it's fatally easy to assume that you could not forget such well-known details, and equally easy to find your mind goes blank at the appropriate time.

Any detail which must be accurate, especially statistical material such as sizes or prices, must be in the cards, as it is easily forgotten and cannot be estimated or guessed. Quotations from someone else's words are also in this category, as are any references which you might need to give. You might like to highlight such information, or write it in a different colour, so that it stands out and can be seen at a glance.

Your main aim in writing notes in this way is to ensure that you give your audience accurate information in the order which seems to you appropriate, but there's a further reason for using cards.

You can write helpful messages to yourself. If you know that you tend to speak too quickly, write 'slow down' in red letters across the top of each card, so that each time you finish with a card and move it to the bottom of the pile, you will again be faced with the message that you must remember. In a margin at the side of each card, mark where the visual aids will come – it's easy to forget a visual aid or to show it too early because of nerves. If you intend to give handout material to the audience at the end of your presentation, write a message at the end of your notes, in a different colour, so that it is there to remind you at the appropriate time.

▶ Timing the presentation

You will have been given a time limit for your presentation, and it's essential that you don't overrun. This is partly a matter of courtesy to the people who follow you, but it is also a sign of professionalism; it may in addition be expedient, as you are likely to lose marks for an overlong talk. It is certainly good practice, as when you make a presentation at work, you will be expected to keep to time or the audience may walk out.

The most important way to make sure that the timing is right is to rehearse until it is. Almost certainly, you will find when you begin to rehearse that you have too much material; you will have to cut it back or redraft it until you are sure that it doesn't exactly fit your time allowance but that you have a little time in hand. It seems to be a rule of presentations that things always take longer than you expect. This is partly the result of audience reaction, for which you may need to pause, and partly because of the natural activity – moving into position, changing a visual aid, changing speakers – which is difficult to estimate in rehearsal. Most of all, it results from the use of the visual aids themselves: the time taken for the audience to see and understand an image on the screen is longer than we tend to allow for (see also page 111).

As a result of all these considerations, you will find that a presentation which is rehearsed to exactly the required 20 minutes will actually take about 23 minutes. This would be a serious mistake, and it's sensible to allow for the extra time: if you are allowed 20 minutes, rehearse to achieve 15 minutes, so that in reality your presentation will probably take 18 minutes, allowing the extra two minutes for any unforeseen interruption. Nobody is likely to worry if you finish a couple of minutes or so before time, and you will give the air of professional control that you want to achieve.

I've discussed the importance of timing in the chapter about notes because you can give yourself extra help by including timing messages on your cards. I mentioned the 'slow down' message; you might also have a 'halfway through' card, which allows you to assess, in a quick glance at the clock or your watch, how the time is going at that point of the presentation. If you have time in hand, there is no problem; if you are running short of time, you will have to leave something out. Plan in advance what you can omit without leaving a serious gap in the argument, and put such material on a different colour card. If you are part of a group presentation, the last speaker will need to plan this with particular care, as he or she is in the unfortunate position of having to adjust the time for everybody else. It's extremely difficult to decide what to leave out while you are actually talking to the audience – such decisions are much better made in advance.

Just before your presentation starts, it can be useful to make a quick note on your cards of the time at which you should end. In theory, this is obvious, but if in practice the previous speaker or group overran, and you began seven minutes later than expected, it can be extraordinarily disconcerting to glance at the clock, see the time at which you expected to finish, and to remember that you have seven minutes left.

It's unlikely, too, that you would remember that the difference is seven minutes unless you made a conscious effort to note it when you began.

Practise with your notes until you are confident in using them, rewriting here or there as necessary. If eventually you feel that you can manage without them, then do so, but rehearse several times without using notes, and make allowance for the fact that you will probably be nervous when you give your presentation, and you may then be very glad for the sense of security they give.

▶ Visual aids

An audience today expects to see visual aids of a high quality. We are used to seeing images which impress, on television, in advertising, in textbooks. If we have to listen for more than a few minutes without anything to look at, we tend to become dissatisfied and restless. A presenter has to be ready to hold the audience's attention not just by words but by appropriate images, indeed, it is difficult to remember a message unless it is reinforced by its visual impact.

This is the primary purpose of visual aids, to supplement the theme of the presentation and to make it more memorable. Visual aids should never be used simply for their striking visual effect or their beauty, or to add variety to the presentation, although they may have all these qualities: they are there as aids to the speaker and must not overwhelm the key message.

Prototypes and demonstrations

Most of this section will be concerned with equipment, but it's worth looking briefly at the use of prototypes and demonstrations. You may want to show a model of your product to your audience: will the audience be able to see it clearly? Is your prototype big enough? Can you mount it on a table, so that people at the back have a better view? Take care, too, that you stand behind it as you introduce it to the audience – it's only too easy to block your own exhibit.

There are extra problems about conducting any kind of demonstration in front of other people. These may be summed up as 'if it can go wrong, it will'. You may go through the process perfectly well just before the audience arrives, but you can never be absolutely sure that things will work as you want them as soon as there are people watching. Nevertheless, for a small audience, it may be a good idea to show what happens, rather than just describing it. Practise, with someone else to help you – it's difficult to keep control of everything yourself. It's useful to persuade someone else to do the practical work, as you describe it, making sure that neither of you is obstructing the view. Don't rush: it takes the audience time to absorb what's happening. Above all, don't panic if it goes wrong; you must be clearly in control and able to continue with the presentation, no matter what unforeseen circumstances arise.

It's almost always wiser to record the demonstration and to use it via the data projector. In that way, you know that the audience will see a successful experiment, and you will maintain control of the visual material at every stage. You will also know that the audience can see what's happening. This is a great advantage of modern technological help with presentations – but there are points to be aware of, as the next sections will show.

As visual aid equipment becomes technically more complex, and the images therefore more intricate or striking, there is an increasing danger that they will themselves become the centre of attention, and that a nervous speaker will try to hide behind them. If this happens, the audience has been cheated: it gave time and perhaps money to hear this speaker, and finds that it could just as well have been sent a video, because there is no personal relationship between speaker and audience. This is the essential rapport in a presentation, and the relationship between audience and screen must always be secondary to it.

In preparing your presentation, then, you have to balance these two needs which the audience will bring to the occasion: the need to see and be helped by visual aids, and the need to build a rapport with you as the speaker. When therefore will it be appropriate for you to show a visual aid? There are innumerable answers to this question, but some of the most common are:

- to introduce yourself and your subject clearly – the 'title page' visual aid;
- to introduce the audience to the various aspects which you will talk about – this will probably be a list of words or short phrases;
- to give an overall picture of your subject before you talk about the detail – a site plan or a picture of the crop you are going to discuss as it grows in the field might come into this category;
- to illustrate some scientific or technical detail which cannot be seen by the naked eye – a leaf structure, for instance;
- to show some process happening as reinforcement of what you are

saying, such as the growth and development of a plant or the movement of air through a building;
- to show relationships, by a simple graph, a hierarchy chart or a flow diagram;
- to show the nature of an object by a three-dimensional illustration or an exploded diagram of its parts.

All these are sensible reasons for using a visual aid, as they reinforce the message by giving additional information which the audience would not be able to gain in any other way. Nevertheless, there are serious limitations to what can be understood and remembered in a visual image: the list above mentioned a 'simple graph', since a complex graph such as might be found in a scientific textbook would be far too detailed for the audience either to see clearly or to absorb. Tabulated figures almost always suffer from the same disadvantage; it's better to choose the figures that really matter and to show these, than to try to put over all the detail of the table.

The audience needs to be able to see clearly and to assimilate everything that it is shown; it also needs to understand why it should take the trouble to do so. The image must therefore be as uncluttered as possible. Too much detail, or too varied a use of colour, makes this difficult; irrelevant information is particularly annoying – this can occur when a visual aid is produced from a printed original which contains material additional to the illustration. The audience often has trouble in reading such detail, and cannot understand its purpose, so that the visual aid loses credibility. For the same reason, 'give-away' details such as a page or a figure number should always be removed.

There are other problems in using printed material as a visual aid. The size of print is almost always much too small (an appropriate size of lettering on the screen is 30 point, and a minimum size is about 22 point ; your report was probably printed in 11 point), and the organisation of the page may be inappropriate for visual effect, for instance, the main point may come near the bottom of the page when it should be about a third of the way down the screen. Assuming that its size is well chosen, this placing should ensure that all the audience, even those at the back, can see it clearly.

Before accepting a visual aid as part of your presentation, check first that it's really needed to help the message. Some information is clear by itself: if the speaker says that 75 per cent of people gave a particular response to a question while a further 25 per cent took the opposite view, the audience will not need to see the figures in order to absorb the message. They will remember these proportions, but would almost certainly forget the exact figures, and this is all that matters. If detailed figures are important, they can be given to the audience in a more suitable form, perhaps as a handout.

The second check is the clarity of the image. Any lettering must be large enough to be seen from the back of the room, the effect must be free of clutter or irrelevant material, and the use of colour must be helpful in clarifying the image.

Colour can be a great problem: it is often forgotten that a high percentage of the male population has some colour defect in their vision (this is rare among women) and a considerable number are completely colour blind, seeing the world more or less as sepia. Obviously, it's not sensible for a presenter to take account of this sad extreme, but there are particular colour combinations which can be avoided, for instance red and green, which are especially difficult to distinguish by anyone with a visual colour defect.

Some colours show up much more clearly than others: use black or dark blue for lettering, and avoid red (which is particularly difficult to see unless it is a large mass of colour), orange or green. There must be sufficient contrast between the foreground and the background colour: yellow or white on dark blue shows up well, but light green on dark green, or pale mauve on a deeper purple, may look acceptable on a computer screen but give insufficient contrast when projected on a large screen.

I mentioned computers. There are only two forms of visual aid in common use nowadays, the rather old-fashioned and low-tech overhead projector (ohp), and the much more up-to-date and complex data projector (sometimes called an LCD projector). During your course, you are likely to use both of these, and we will discuss their advantages, disadvantages and ease of use in more detail. However, it's important to check what is available in your own department, and to take the appropriate action; ohps are probably widely available, but you may have to reserve a data projector a week or two before your presentation, as they are much less common, and much more expensive.

The overhead projector
The ohp may be looked down on nowadays, but it has great advantages: it's easy to use, can be moved with little trouble, and is unlikely to break down; transparencies can be made cheaply, are easy to transport, and can look effective. Make your transparencies by photocopying onto the right sort of acetate (as long as the original is clear

enough), or by printing directly onto acetate (again, the right sort) from the computer. Hand-drawn transparencies look highly unprofessional.

Even with such a simple form of visual aid, you need to consider the comfort of the audience. An ohp switched on without an acetate in place produces an uncomfortable glare: always put your transparency in position before switching on. 'Fringe glare' or distortion can occur at the edges of the picture; correct this by using the control, or, if this is impossible, position the projector wherever it gives less distortion. If the problem is 'keystoning', when the top of the image is wider than the bottom, tilt the screen, and again move the projector around to find the best position. Avoid a bright light falling onto the screen – the ohp can stand ordinary room lighting, but sunlight directly on the screen will 'fade' the image. The fan of an ohp is often noisy, and while you can't eliminate this, make sure that your voice can be clearly heard over it.

As with any visual aid, limit the amount of information to the most important points. If the image is crowded, the audience will find it difficult to assimilate the information that really matters. Avoid long sentences – key points are usually more effective – and check that the main message is towards the top centre of the screen. If the writing stretches towards the bottom of the transparency, it may be hidden from view by the projector itself. Remember that the lettering must be large enough for everyone to see, and use a natural mixture of upper and lower case letters – text in capital letters is harder to read. Choose a sans-serif font, to keep the image as simple and uncluttered as possible.

Always use the computer spellcheck before printing onto the acetate. Spelling errors projected onto a large screen distract the audience for as long as they are in view.

In using the ohp, there are techniques which you need to remember:

- Check that you stand clear of the audience's sight-lines: stand back, alongside the screen, so that you can see it and the audience at the same time.
- Use a pointer, and point to the screen, not on the projector; you will need to point to the important aspects of diagrams on the screen, but hardly ever to words, which the audience can read for themselves.
- Always glance quickly at the screen to check that the image is straight and in focus.
- Don't switch the ohp on and off repeatedly, or the bulb may blow; it

isn't necessary to switch off when you simply change the transparency, but don't leave an image on the screen when you have finished discussing it.

- Allow the audience time to assimilate the whole message on the screen – don't be tempted to start talking while they are still reading. Watch them to see when they stop looking at the screen and look back at you.
- The 'progressive revelation' technique, much used by some lecturers, is not recommended. It's difficult to get it right, and audiences tend to perceive it as patronising. Use overlays of acetate if you need to build up an image.

If you remember these points, you will find little difficulty in using the ohp effectively; the same is not necessarily true, unfortunately, of the data projector.

The data projector

The most high-tech, up-to-date visual aid equipment in common use is probably the data projector; as presenters frequently use PowerPoint to prepare their material, the term 'PowerPoint presentation' is often used to mean the whole presentation, including the use of a laptop computer and a data projector. This equipment is expensive and has to be treated with care, but if it's used sensibly, it can be very effective.

Perhaps the first, and in many ways the most important comment about this equipment is its ability to go wrong at the critical moment. Whenever you use it, be sure that you have backup available; interestingly, the ohp has had a new lease of life as the appropriate equipment to use when you find that the data projector isn't going to work. As transparencies can be created in advance on PowerPoint and printed off onto acetate, the effect can often be just as acceptable as using anything more up to date. When you find that your laptop is not compatible with the projector, or the software won't run on the equipment provided, or you are networked to a different site, or the whole system has crashed, you need to be able to give your presentation in just as professional a way as if everything had gone smoothly. Always have backup.

There is another decision which presenters often face. You have set up your equipment, and the audience has arrived; you are ready to start, but you can't boot up your computer. Something is wrong, and you start to use the keyboard with increasing frustration in an attempt to produce the material you so carefully prepared. The audience is sympathetic – up to a point. There is a limit to the time you can keep them sitting there waiting when nothing is happening. You are, of course, also losing precious presentation time. Be ready to make the decision to stop, smile at the audience, tell them that the problem can't be overcome quickly, but that you are going to start your presentation, using your backup visual material. They will be relieved and also impressed that you had prepared for any difficulty, and that there is therefore nothing for them to worry about. As long as you are clearly calm and in control, the audience will give you credit for coping with the situation.

In preparing your material, you will need to take account of many of the points made earlier about the ohp. Size of print in a sans-serif font, amount on the screen, sensible use of colour, are all the same, but there are extra considerations. You may be using a light background colour with a darker form for the print, for instance dark blue print on a pale blue background. This can look very effective, but you always need to check the image on the large screen. The colour contrast may look adequate on the monitor, but be totally inadequate when the image is projected.

Backgrounds on offer in the package you are using can also cause problems. In many ways, it is safer to use a plain colour background than to choose something more elaborate and then find that the audience is distracted. Waving palm trees or pretty patterns like wallpaper are inappropriate in a scientific or technical presentation. Even patterns which seem discreet can have an undesirable effect; if the depth of colour varies across the screen you may inadvertently give more emphasis to some words than to others. If your chosen background includes a stripe of red at one side of the screen, this may look like underlining, and so draw attention to a point which is no more important than anything else on the screen. Again, the answer is to project your images and then look at them critically to see if there is any effect which might distract the audience from your main message.

Movement on the screen can also divert the audience. It is too easy to have points in a list appearing from the sides of the screen, or rising from the bottom, or moving around, when no purpose is served by this activity. If you need to show movement, then the data projector allows you to do so efficiently, but if the movement has no significance, it is better avoided. It may be more effective to show the audience the whole picture than to build up the list one item at a time – it depends, as always, on your message. As with any other form of visual aid, the data projector must support the speaker, and not become a distraction.

In spite of these warnings, there are obvious advantages in using this equipment. You can, if you need to do so, incorporate sound, slides, a moving image or a three-dimensional illustration, and all this is under the control of the one piece of equipment. Information can be updated or corrections made at the last minute. Moving the image on is simple, whether you use a mouse, the keyboard or the remote control. You also give an impression of being up to date in your thinking, as you are clearly up to date with your visual material. However, there's a danger that you will be so impressed by the possibilities, and so intent on making a good impression with them, that you don't allow enough time to prepare what you want to say. Don't allow the visual material to take over too much of your preparation time or attention.

In using the data projector, there are points to remember:

- Check the lighting in the room. You may need to dim the front lights, or to draw a blind.

- The audience will need just as long to read the words on the screen, or to assimilate the details of a diagram, as they do when you're using an ohp. Stand back, check the image on the screen, and don't move on until the audience is ready. You may find it easier to leave the remote control or the mouse on the table rather than in your hand; this helps you to pace your talk, and also avoids the danger of accidentally moving the image on without noticing. Use a pointer on the screen to help the audience to focus on the detail of diagrams.

- Don't try to hide behind the equipment. You should not be sitting at your laptop, you should be standing up and looking at the audience.

- Consider turning the monitor off, or moving it away, before you begin. There's a temptation to look at it too often, or even to watch it as you speak, and then you're not looking at the audience.

- You may need to show an image again in answer to a question. Make sure that you can do this easily, perhaps by having a printout of all your visual material available, or use one of your backup ohp transparencies.

- Use a blank screen if you are moving on but have no image to show immediately – don't leave the audience looking at irrelevant material. As with any visual material, don't overwhelm the audience: your visuals are there to serve you, not the other way round.

Try out your visual aid equipment, and be familiar with it at the rehearsal stage. Think about where it will be positioned, ensuring that there is plenty of space for you. Rehearse with your visual material, so that you are at ease with it – some presenters look at the screen with evident surprise, as if they've never seen the image before. Perhaps they haven't, but this does nothing to inspire confidence in the audience. Above all, view your visuals as your servants: they must be good quality and they must support what you are saying. But the most important relationship is between you, the speaker, and your audience.

► Key points

- ► Don't read from a full text when you are speaking to an audience; make sure that you use 'spoken' language
- ► You can use your own visual aids as your notes, or prompt cards. Write out words and phrases only, not sentences
- ► Use your notes to help with the timing, and include any other helpful messages to yourself
- ► Prepare visual aids in the light of the subject and the needs of the audience, and ensure that everyone can see them clearly
- ► Know why you are using colour, choose a sans-serif font, and limit the amount of detail on each image
- ► The more technically advanced the equipment, the more likely it is to go wrong. If you use a computer, always have backup
- ► Try out your equipment in advance, and be familiar with it and, if possible, with the room in which you will make your presentation

7 Delivery and Non-verbal Communication

Thorough preparation is essential to a good presentation; the last two chapters have discussed the various stages which need to be completed, whether by a group or by an individual speaker. This chapter considers the presentation itself: assuming that presenters are well prepared, how can they ensure that they make an appropriate impact on the audience?

The key is a professional approach. It isn't easy to define professionalism, but it has to do with confidence, with appearance, with a high standard of material, both spoken and visual, and with mutual trust – the speaker relies on the courtesy and attention of the audience, and the audience relies on the speaker to provide interesting and useful information in an efficient way. This trust is absolutely essential for a successful presentation, indeed, if it is lacking, the presentation will be a failure in spite of any amount of technical skill on the part of the speaker.

▶ First appearances

The initial impact of speaker on audience is visual. The presenter comes into view and the audience makes a quick assessment – reasonably enough, as they have given up precious time to come and listen. I have already mentioned the importance of appropriate dress (see page 111); brightly coloured clothing or ostentatious jewellery will distract from the message and will suggest a less than formal approach. At the audience's first glance, they must see that the speaker looks right for the occasion.

It is more than just a question of dress. A confident walk, a smile at the audience, obvious awareness of where to sit or stand – all these things help the audience to sense a professional approach. If you shuffle in, head down, wearing a miserable expression on your face, you will have put the audience off before you say a word.

At this point, you (one of you, in a group presentation) will have to make a quick assessment of any necessary last minute adjustments. You will, of course, have checked out the room and the equipment in advance, but chairs can be moved; an earlier speaker might have moved a projector so that it is no longer in focus, you may need to set up your own equipment or to boot up the computer – all these activities take time, although careful rehearsal will shorten that time considerably. Prepare or check these details before you start to speak. It is much easier to keep the audience waiting for a minute or two while you refocus the projector than to have to stop your presentation when you suddenly realise that what you are showing is out of focus and must be put right.

Check the position of the furniture, and don't hesitate to move anything which could present a problem. Speakers have been known to walk round a chair at regular intervals while they are speaking, apparently never thinking that it could be moved out of their way. Previous speakers may have stood at the (audience) right-hand side of the screen, but if you are left-handed, you may be more comfortable at the other side – if that means moving a table out of the way, then move it. All these considerations can be dealt with easily and quickly before you begin to speak, and they will then cease to be potential or actual problems. What is more, the audience will admire your foresight and confidence, in a word, your professionalism.

Your first words of greeting are addressed to the whole audience, and should be spoken out clearly, accompanied by a smile and eye contact with as many people as possible. We will discuss these aspects of non-verbal communication later in the chapter (see page 142), but it is worth stressing here that this initial greeting is enormously important. The audience must feel that you want to be there talking to them – whether this is true or not. When you look at them, they feel that you have come for their benefit; when you smile at them, they feel that you want to build a good relationship with them, and when you say 'Good morning, ladies and gentlemen', or, slightly less formally, 'Good morning, everyone', you are building on that courtesy and know that they can hear you without difficulty. You are already creating an air of professionalism, long before you reach the scientific part of your talk.

▶ Using your nerves

You are very likely to be nervous at the prospect of giving a presentation to members of your department, and rightly so. If you are lucky, you will continue to feel nervous on such occasions, even when you are very senior in your company and making presentations to professional institutions or to your organisation's clients. The most important point to remember about nerves is that they are undoubtedly and always a good thing.

What does the audience think, when they see that the speaker is nervous? First of all, they are vastly relieved that it is someone else who is giving the presentation – 'Better him than me' is a common reaction. Second, they are rather flattered. Clearly, the occasion matters to the speaker; their reactions are important; the presenter cares about them and about the message. These are good signs to be sending out, and the audience will feel them as such, always provided that your nerves don't overwhelm you.

If you are overconfident, the audience will see that very quickly, too. The message this time is that you are (too) sure of yourself, that you don't really care what the audience thinks, that you are giving the presentation solely for your own benefit. No audience likes to be treated in this way, and they will soon start to react badly to you. By the time you reach the questions, there may well be a feeling that it would be no bad thing to catch you out, and you may find that the questions are hostile and aggressive in tone.

All these are obviously signs of a bad relationship between speaker and audience; you are concerned to build a good relationship which is mutually beneficial. So be glad that you are nervous – it is a strong point in your favour.

There is another reason to be pleased about your nerves. When we are nervous, we get a flow of adrenaline which makes us react more quickly. As a result, our brains work rapidly, we may remember information which we hardly realised we knew, and we can think at speed about how to cope with a difficulty, should one arise.

The flow of adrenaline itself has another good effect. It adds a pleasurable tension to the occasion. The pleasure, oddly, works for both speaker and audience: it is not uncommon for student presenters to say 'I was very scared before I started, but once I got going, to my surprise I quite enjoyed myself', and for an audience to say 'The topic sounded rather dry, but they made it really interesting, quite exciting, in fact.' The tension flows between speaker and audience, and both, once they get used to it, find a sense of occasion, of excitement, which is itself pleasurable.

The very worst way to react when you are nervous is to worry about your nerves. The more you think about them, the worse they will get, until they begin to inhibit your thinking, and you start to lose the sense of what you are saying. It is much better to accept your nerves and to think of the benefits they bring: 'I'm nervous, of course, but so what? It's a good thing I am' is a sensible approach to the presentation.

Nevertheless, nerves can be a nuisance if they are allowed to be so, and you need to be aware of ways of controlling them. The first is, of course, thorough preparation of your material, so that you are totally familiar with it, and are sure that it is both well chosen and correct. Second, rehearsals will help you, as you will become increasingly at ease with the words and the visual aids, and reasonably sure that nothing will take you by surprise. It's particularly helpful to rehearse at least once in the setting in which you will be giving your presentation, as the sense of having been there before removes some of the strangeness and the stress. It also gives you the chance to become familiar with the equipment, the lighting of the room and so on.

You are trying to forestall problems that might arise. If you suddenly find that you can't operate the projector, of course this will increase your nerves, as will the absence of blackout when you want to use slides or the data projector (see pages 127–30), or the awful realisation that you forgot to make a slide which you now need. All such difficulties can be prevented if you rehearse fully in the appropriate room. There may, of course, be problems which you couldn't foresee, such as the projector bulb blowing, but even then, if you know how to get a spare and fit it, the accident won't totally destroy your confidence.

Confidence is the key word. It can exist side by side with nerves, and indeed should do so. 'I'm nervous, but I'm also confident' is a good frame of mind for a presenter, and much better than 'I'm good at this, so I don't have to worry.' (More advice about controlling nerves is given in the section about breathing, page 135.)

▶ **Using your voice effectively**

Once the presentation has started, the speaker has to use two principal attributes: the voice and non-verbal communication (body language). Both are important if there is to be a proper rapport between speaker and audience. Those who listen must, of course, be able to hear without strain, and the first and essential aspect of using the voice is that it should be loud enough, clear enough, and well paced.

Volume

It's useful to ask yourself about your own voice. Do you think that it's too loud or too soft or about right? It's very unlikely that your voice is too loud; although it happens occasionally that people overmodulate for a given space (generally the effect of trying to shout rather than project the voice), it is far more common that people speak too quietly. If you feel that this is a problem, ask yourself why. Do you dislike the idea of presenting to an audience so much that you want to hide from them, physically and vocally? Think that a close friend is sitting at the back of the audience, a focus for what you want to say. Forget that other people will be there, and try in rehearsal to communicate with this one friend – you need to look at your friend, and then to throw your voice as far as you can.

There are other voice exercises that may help you. Say very loudly some of the explosive sounds, such as 'Bang!', 'Stop!' and 'Crash!' Shout them as loud as you can, and notice how you use your mouth in doing so. Get a sense of your voice filling the space. Now try to say the words rather than shout them, moving your mouth in the same way.

You may be swallowing your voice, keeping it too far towards the back of your throat. Try humming a tune, and see how your voice is forward, in the mask of your face rather than in your throat. Humming is good, too, for breathing practice. Take a good, deep breath, filling your diaphragm rather than just your chest space. Now hum a single note for as long as you can, on the same breath. If you run out of breath in twenty seconds or less, you aren't breathing deeply enough, or controlling your breath properly (or you smoke). Put your hands on the front of your rib cage, and make sure that you can feel the air intake there; shallow breathing may be part of your problem. Practise each day, extending the length of time that you can hum on the one breath. Sometimes, for a change, start your humming and then gradually get louder, and then softer again. You are beginning to control your breathing, which is essential for public speaking. Usefully, you are also learning to handle your nerves, as deep, controlled breathing relaxes the body and so, automatically, the mind. Try to breathe deeply and slowly the next time you feel stressed, and you will immediately feel more relaxed and able to cope.

Your voice is supported by your breath, which, from a speaking point of view, is why it's so important to breathe properly. Once you are used to breathing from your diaphragm, try squeezing your diaphragm muscles gently. It's much like squeezing a tube of toothpaste at the bottom – toothpaste (or in this case more sound) comes out at the top. You can increase your volume in this way without shouting, which is unpleasant to listen to and harms the vocal chords.

None of these or similar exercises will give you a loud voice straight-away, and you will need to keep up the practice. In the meantime, try to do a bit of public speaking, even if it's only a couple of minutes to a friend, and put your breathing work into action. Remember that it will help you if you look at the audience; stand up, and make sure that your feet point towards them, so that you can't turn away and hide again. Don't look at the screen or the projector while you're talking. A certain amount of hearing is actually lip-reading; it's important for listeners to be able to see the speaker's face. Imagine that you had in the audience someone who is profoundly deaf (it could happen). That person must see your face, and is dependent upon your lip movements. Make sure that you articulate as clearly and precisely as you can; above all, don't mutter. Even if your voice is still soft, you are giving your audience as much help as possible.

Pace

The speed at which you speak is almost as important for audibility as the volume you use. Think again about your own voice. Do you think that it's too slow? This is unlikely; it's very difficult to speak too slowly to an audience, although what occasionally happens is that the speaker breaks up the flow of words with pauses in unnecessary places. Take as an example part of the introduction to a presentation:

> Our presentation will last for about twenty minutes after which we'll be happy to answer your questions.

This sentence will include two pauses, the more important of which is indicated by the comma; there is also a very slight pause after the word 'about', as the next word, twenty, is a number. Numbers are notoriously difficult to hear, and always need to be emphasised, usually by a tiny pause. The speaker whose voice tends to be too slow will introduce other pauses:

> Our presentation ... will last for about ... twenty minutes ... after which we'll be happy ... to answer your questions.

The problem with this disjointed form of speech is that the audience doesn't know where it's going; they have no sense of a continuing message, and, especially when the material becomes complex, will soon lose the thread of the argument. Incidentally, that useful little pause before 'twenty' no longer helps – the pauses are too frequent to create any feeling of emphasis.

However, slow speech is a rare problem; rapid speech is all too common, and is a much more serious handicap from the audience's point of view. Words run together and can't be clearly distinguished, sentences aren't separated and so become too complicated to be absorbed, and worst of all, the audience has no breathing time in which to assimilate the information.

Pauses are an essential part of a presentation. Think of a good lecturer, one from whom you find it easy to take notes. Almost certainly he or she will pause to let you catch up, will stop for a minute or two to let you consider a difficult point, and will use pauses for emphasis so that you know at once what is especially worth remembering. You need to incorporate these techniques into your presenting skills. There are moments in a presentation which lend themselves naturally to silence.

You are changing a visual aid, and for a few seconds your attention is removed from the audience; they are watching your actions rather than listening. You need to be silent. The visual aid is presented, and the audience looks at it with interest; they aren't listening to you. If you ask them to look and to listen at the same time, they will face a small crisis, and will almost certainly resolve it by looking – the visual impact usually dominates. You have finished speaking, and your colleague is getting ready to continue the presentation; there will be a pause. You want to emphasise an important point, or to give a piece of numerical information, and you do so by pausing very slightly. You may even, if it seems wise, try a touch of humour (see page 144), and the audience laughs; you wait for them to stop laughing and settle down before continuing. As you move from one aspect of your topic to another, you register the change of direction by a small pause, to allow the audience to appreciate what is happening. In the unlikely event of your forgetting what you are going to say next, you will simply pause for a few seconds while you look at your notes. This last pause is particularly important: if you start to look anxious, and mutter 'erm', 'er' or such-like, the audience immediately knows that there's a problem; if you simply pause, they will assume that it's a pause for effect and won't even realise what is happening.

A presentation is full of pauses, for one reason or another, and they are needed by the audience. If you talk non-stop, the audience will become bewildered, will lose its way, and eventually will give up the attempt to follow what you are saying. Pauses, in addition to all their other benefits, give the audience time to think.

If you speak too quickly, you are probably not allowing sufficient silence; if you make a pause, you will also probably start to speak again a little more slowly, just because there has been an interruption.

Think about your overall rate of speech. Do you know how quickly you speak? In ordinary conversation, you probably talk at a rate of something like 160 words a minute (remember that you may well read at 400–500 words a minute – see page 115). When you are talking to an audience, you will need to slow right down to something like 110–120 words a minute, depending a little on the size of your audience. Try this, by choosing a passage of about 250 words, and reading it out loud, trying to make it last for at least two minutes. It will seem very strange and unnatural at first, but this is about the right speed for public speaking. Use a cassette recorder, and record yourself speaking as slowly as you can, and compare your speed with that of a very good speaker, perhaps on the radio.

Your colleagues will also be able to help. When you are rehearsing together, ask them to stop you as soon as you start to rush, or your words are indistinct. Use your notes to help, as suggested earlier (page 120). Try to move a bit more slowly; sometimes people are pushed along by their own rapid movement, in walking into position or changing a visual aid. Your speed is, after all, closely associated with the timing of the presentation; if you have selected an appropriate amount of material for the time available, it would be a pity to spoil the effect by getting through it in half the time!

Variety in your voice

I've stressed the importance of speaking clearly, with sufficient volume, allowing pauses, and speaking slowly. When all these factors are under control, it's worth looking at the extent to which you vary your voice.

This is partly a matter of emphasis. As you make a particularly important point, you need to slow down even more and increase your volume very slightly. You may also make one of the tiny pauses which I mentioned earlier, before and maybe also after, this key message. In doing so, you are letting the audience know that this is something to which they should pay especial attention, without telling them so in words. When you move on to an example, or an additional piece of lesser information, speed up slightly and pull back a little on the volume. The audience will get the message, and you will be achieving variety in your voice.

Don't be afraid of a touch of drama. There is much in common between acting and public speaking, and although there are also obvious differences, you can employ some of an actor's techniques, such as holding back an important detail for a few seconds in order to draw the audience's attention to it, or allowing your tone and your voice to combine in emphasising what you are saying. Try saying an expression such as 'It's surprising that', and see what happens when you say the word 'surprising'. Your eyebrows will rise, your eyes will open wide, and you will look surprised. We allow this non-verbal communication to happen in ordinary life, and it is perfectly acceptable in a presentation.

▶ Non-verbal communication (body language)

It's virtually impossible to communicate by our voices alone; this is true even if we're speaking by telephone. The recipient of our message can't see us, but we still choose the way we sit in response to the person we're talking to – upright if it's our head of department, lounging if it's a friend. Think of giving directions over the phone; you will probably indicate a left turn with your hand, or even make a circular movement when you mention a roundabout. Such body language is a normal part of our everyday life, but people are sometimes inhibited about using it when they are speaking to an audience. If you react like this, you are robbing other people of an essential source of information.

There is a very important consideration about body language, which I must stress before I discuss its use in any detail: body language is closely allied to culture, and what is acceptable to one nationality may be unacceptable, even offensive, to another. If you are speaking abroad, or if your audience is of a different nationality, always check with your contact before you prepare to speak, asking whether there is anything you should particularly avoid or add to your normal response. We can't change our non-verbal communication totally, because it is so deeply ingrained in our personalities, but we can modify it a little if it seems wise to do so. In this chapter, I have assumed a Western European background to the presentation; if this isn't right in your case, you must check all that I say and find out how appropriate it is for you.

I have already shown how we use facial expression to show emotion, in stressing the importance of smiling at the audience at the beginning of the presentation. We are registering our welcome and our willingness to talk to them. Interestingly, human beings often 'shadow' each other: if two friends are talking, they may unconsciously adopt an identical posture. When we smile at the audience, they are likely to smile back, which gives us the bonus of starting to speak to a friendly looking group. If we look dismal at the prospect of speaking to them, they will be likely to look back with a similar expression, and we have to start speaking to an apparently miserable audience.

Using your hands

Some people use their hands more than others while they are speaking; it's important not to have fidgety movements or to fiddle with your hair or the pointer, but a controlled use of the hands can be effective. As I've said, we use them to indicate messages such as directions; we show size or height with our hands, or rapid movement, and all such indications emphasise the words we are speaking.

Sometimes we gesture towards the audience as a means of including them in what we're saying. 'You will all be aware that ... ' involves the audience, and we often add a gesture, such as opening our hands and moving them slightly towards those who are listening. In our culture, a closed fist always signifies aggression, while an open hand suggests friendliness and generosity.

Check, when you are rehearsing, that you have no natural hand gesture which would seem irritating or odd to an audience. Rubbing your hands together or holding your notes high in front of your chest makes you look strange and ill at ease; people sometimes develop very distracting habits such as unbuttoning a jacket and then buttoning it up again, repeatedly. The pointer can cause trouble: speakers extend and contract it unnecessarily, fiddle with it until it disintegrates, or keep it extended and wave it around so that they look as if they are taking part in a fencing match or conducting an orchestra.

Body movement

It isn't only hands which can be used to show that the audience is included; there may be moments when the speaker wants to lean slightly forward or move a pace towards them. Words such as 'You will all agree ... ', or 'We are sure that you will want to buy our product' suggest a forward movement towards those who are going to agree, or to buy the product. If at such moments the speaker moves back, there is an odd sense of conflict: the words suggest a good relationship – you will buy from us – but the body language suggests that the speaker actually wants to put a greater space between seller and buyer, that, in spite of the words, there is a deteriorating relationship between them.

Body language is immensely powerful. It may even override all that we are saying. 'We are happy to answer your questions', spoken brightly and positively, suggests that the speaker is really happy; spoken with a miserable look and a retreating movement, the same words create exactly the opposite impression.

Using the feet

Our feet can be a great nuisance during a presentation. Speakers sometimes shuffle as they first move into position; they shift their weight regularly from one foot to the other; they walk in a rhythmical way backwards and forwards; they rock, either to and fro or from side to side; or their feet go together as if they were glued, and keep their owners standing to attention as if on guard duty.

All such movement, or unnatural lack of movement, is distracting and may become irritating. The best way to stand during a presentation is with your feet slightly apart and the weight evenly balanced between them. If you stand like that, you are unlikely to sway or rock to and fro, and you look reasonably at ease. If you stand to attention, you won't look at ease and there is a distinct possibility that you will start to sway.

Don't try to stand still all the time; it isn't natural, and makes you look tense and inhibited. You need a small area which is your own: your colleagues and the equipment should be outside this space, and in it you should be able to move freely. Move towards the audience when it seems right to do so; move back to the screen when you want to use the pointer (see page 126). Experienced speakers allow themselves a good deal of freedom to move during a presentation, without fidgeting or creating a pattern of regular movement.

When you are sitting down in front of the audience and one of your colleagues is speaking, your feet still need to be under control. They should not tie themselves in knots, or describe circles in the air. Sit well back in your chair, in an upright position, and keep your feet on the ground. If you start to tap your foot, you are signalling impatience or irritation, and the audience will immediately wonder why. This question will interest them and hold their attention when they should be listening to and looking at the speaker.

Eye contact

In a Western European culture, the single most important aspect of body language is eye contact. You absolutely must look at the audience. In the English language, there is a word reserved almost entirely for people who won't meet other people's eyes during a conversation: they are seen as shifty. The overtones of this word are untrustworthy, not telling the truth, probably not themselves believing what they're saying – exactly the opposite of the trusting relationship needed between audience and speaker.

Don't try to escape eye contact. Sometimes people say that you can look along the hairlines of the listeners, or just between them, but this is bad advice. The audience will soon notice, and will feel that you are avoiding them. As you move forward with your greeting at the start of your talk, deliberately try to make eye contact with as many people as possible. You may not be able to see everyone, especially if there is a big audience and the lighting has been dimmed, but at least look towards those who are sitting near the back, so they feel that you are including them. If you do this, you will find that you have good eye contact throughout your presentation; if you avoid people's gaze at the start, you will find it increasingly difficult to make eye contact as you continue to speak.

Some positions are especially difficult. You will have checked that you are standing where everyone can see you, but if there are members of the audience to your right and left, it's easy to neglect them, as they will be outside your natural field of vision. Try to turn round to look at them from time to time. Don't stand too much to one side of the speaking area if you can possibly avoid it, as it will encourage you to look at the people diagonally opposite you and to ignore those closest to you.

Eye contact must be very brief. If you hold contact for too long, the person you are looking at will start to look embarrassed and probably laugh, and you will want to laugh in response – a distraction to you both. It should be as natural to look at the audience during a presentation as it is to look at a group of friends you are talking to and, with practice, it will seem just as automatic.

The response of the audience

Non-verbal communication is a two-way process. You are sending all sorts of messages to your audience, and they are responding. One reason why it is so essential that you look at your audience (for more ideas about eye contact, see the section above), is that you must be able to judge their response and, if appropriate, react to it.

Tapping the foot is an obvious sign; folding the arms and frowning shows a similar irritation, or perhaps profound disagreement with what the speaker is saying. There is little that the speaker can do immediately, but it's worth noting that this has happened and that there are likely to be hostile questions about what you've just said. Audience body language can produce an immediate reaction: if some of the audience are leaning sideways and obviously trying and failing to see the screen, then the speaker must move out of the way. Looking at watches, putting papers in briefcases and whispering to neighbours suggests that the speaker is overrunning and had better conclude quickly. Leaning right back in the seat and looking out of the window is harder for the speaker to deal with, but such actions do suggest that there is something wrong – perhaps that the audience is bored. Why is this happening? There may be nothing to be done at the time, but the speaker can think about it for the future.

On the other hand, the problem may not be the speaker's, and this is something that it's hard to recognise while you're speaking. Audiences can react awkwardly at first because they are still recovering from the previous (awful) presentation. Some may have to give presentations after you, and they are nervous and finding it hard to concentrate. Someone may have had an argument earlier in the day, and it is still interrupting their thoughts. Speakers often feel that the very worst thing that could happen is that someone in the audience will go to sleep. If they do, how do you know that it isn't the result of feeling unwell, having had a sleepless night, or jet-lag?

Speakers inevitably tend to blame themselves, and this can affect the rest of the presentation. If there is a general reaction against what you are saying, you may face a problem, but if it's only one or two people, perhaps the others agree with you; perhaps you're right. If people look sleepy, maybe the room is too stuffy. If something goes wrong, put it right and then forget it. If you drop your notes, you may feel terrible at the time, but if you pick them up, sort them quickly and carry on, the chances are that by the end of your presentation nobody except you will remember the incident. The important message is that the speaker is in charge and can influence what happens. If you refuse to allow yourself to be distracted, and carry on to the best of your ability, the audience will probably forget what happened or if they remember, they will be sympathetic. You will lose their goodwill only if you panic, seem embarrassed or fail to carry on in a professional way.

▶ **Using humour**

Laughter is useful as a way of making people feel at home with one another, but in a presentation it can be dangerous. Examine any humour which you are thinking of introducing: does it arise naturally from what you are saying? It mustn't be an 'add-on' joke; you want the audience to take you seriously as a professional, not as a comedian. Could it possibly upset or offend anyone in the audience? There is a great deal that we don't know about people just by looking at them, and we must be absolutely sure that we don't alienate anybody listening. When we're sure about these aspects, we must then be certain that if we do use humour, we can put it over well. A joke that falls absolutely flat should never have been tried; some people have a natural ability to time a line well, and others haven't. If you belong to the second category, leave humour well alone.

This advice makes one thing clear: off the cuff humour rarely has a place in a presentation. If you are highly experienced, totally at ease with the audience and the situation, and far too senior to have anything to lose if it doesn't work, then you might think of a witty remark on the spur of the moment and risk saying it. But a risk is still what you're taking.

▶ **Answering questions**

I talked earlier about the need to identify questions and plan the answers, as an essential aspect of your preparation. How you give the answers is equally important to the total effect on the audience, and body language is involved in this, too.

There are different types of questioner. Some, sadly, will be present simply to shine at your expense; they are much less interested in what you have to say than in giving their own opinion. If you stay in academic life, you will find that such people are sometimes found at conferences. Together with this unpleasant group, we can put those who are aggressive in their questioning, trying to make you feel ill at ease. You are unlikely to meet either of these categories in an undergraduate setting, but it is not impossible.

There are two golden rules: should you find people like this in your audience, be impeccably courteous to them at all times, and use the rest of the audience – which is likely to be on your side – to help you. Think about the body language of your questioner. Hostility makes us move towards our opponent, sometimes too close for their comfort, enforcing close eye contact; we pull our eyebrows into a frown, tense up our shoulders and use our hands fiercely, perhaps jabbing with a finger. These are the responses which must be avoided. Take a deep breath, relax your shoulders, make sure that your hands are quietly by your side, and smile – you are showing your opponent that you are not disturbed by what has been said, and the rest of the audience that you are calm and in control. Answer briefly and politely, and then break free of the close eye contact. Step back, look round at the rest of the audience, and ask if anyone else has a comment to make or a question to ask. You will be breaking the potentially dangerous link between you and your opponent; the situation will be diffused by your actions, and you will have created a good impression on the main part of your audience.

If you can't hear the question, ask for it to be repeated. If you still can't hear, take the responsibility on yourself or place it firmly on the room ('the acoustics of this room are difficult, aren't they?') and either answer the question that you think you are being asked, or offer to talk to the questioner personally afterwards. This latter response is useful if the question is irrelevant or unclear even after it has been repeated. If you don't know the answer, say so (see also page 108), but if you can find the answer afterwards, offer to do so. Remain calm and courteous throughout, and you will retain audience goodwill.

▶ Improving your presentation skills

You may be inexperienced at public speaking, nervous and afraid of doing something wrong. If you have read this chapter, you will have a lot of good advice, but you may doubt whether you can remember it all when the moment arrives. Don't allow yourself to worry too much about this, lessening whatever confidence you have and increasing the risk of panic.

The secret is to identify any particular problem which you know is hampering your ability to speak well. Perhaps you speak too quickly. In rehearsal, concentrate on speaking more slowly, and ask a friend to stop you as soon as you start to speed up. Add helpful comments to your notes (see page 120). Then when you are at last in front of the audience, don't worry about your speed. Much good practice in making presentations comes from developing good habits, and if you have worked hard at the problem in rehearsal, you will have started the good habit of speaking more slowly. You may not yet have got your pace absolutely right, but it is better than it was, and it will be better still next time. Making professional presentations is a skill which can be learnt, although it is undoubtedly easier for some people than for others; the advice given in this book will help you, but in the end you will learn to make presentations by making them and – as most people find – getting better all the time.

▶ Key points

- ▶ A presentation depends on mutual trust between speaker and audience. Make sure that the first impression you give is appropriately professional
- ▶ Make eye contact and smile at the audience as you greet them
- ▶ Nerves are a good thing. Be nervous, but rehearse until you are also confident
- ▶ Work on your voice until you can control the volume and the pace at which you speak; remember the value of silence
- ▶ Use appropriate body language; don't fidget, but don't try to keep too still. Eye contact with the audience is essential throughout your presentation
- ▶ Beware of humour: if it works, it can be most effective, but if it falls flat, you will have difficulty in regaining the audience's attention and your own confidence
- ▶ Think in advance about possible questions and how you will answer them. Take your time, and be courteous to the audience under all circumstances
- ▶ The more presentations you give, the better presenter you will become

8 Surviving the Viva

From an early stage of your course, you will probably have to make presentations; later, as the work becomes more complex and your own knowledge and experience develop, you may be involved with other forms of oral examination, such as a viva (a short, formal, assessed interview between two or more members of staff and an individual student), or a project interview (also sometimes called a viva, which follows the completion of a project and project report); some subjects require other forms of presentation, such as the poster presentation (common in the pure sciences) and the walk-through (in computer sciences).

Currently, there is a heated debate about the value of such occasions, not only between institutions but also between faculties and departments. Some have done away with any form of oral assessment, while others require every student to take part in at least one form of viva. This book is not concerned with the debate itself, although one point is perhaps worth making: if you are working as a professional scientist or engineer in a company, you will be involved with team briefings, meetings with clients, papers and discussions at meetings or conferences, and day-to-day conversations with your colleagues and your managers. Any experience which will help you to perform more creditably on such occasions will be good for your career, and from this point of view at least, vivas have some value.

In this chapter, I will look in some detail at the two most common forms of oral assessment, the formal viva which may well be part of your final examination, and the project interview which will conclude a project on which you have been working and about which you will have written a report. One or two other forms of presentation will also be discussed more briefly. There is wide variation, as well as debate, between the practice of different departments, and you are advised to find out exactly what form any such assessment will take in your own section or department, and what weight will be given to the result.

▶ **The viva**

Some courses include a viva as a matter of routine, and all students take part; in other cases, perhaps the majority, vivas are required for particular students under specific circumstances, as shown below.

1. Every student who has failed final examinations: this is an attempt to be fair to such a student; perhaps there was some reason for the failure which has not been recognised. There is usually a real desire to give any possible credit, and to allow the student to present himself or herself in the best possible light. The viva will probably have a broad base, asking about the way in which the student has tackled the course, and advice might be given about a possible next step in the circumstances.

2. Students who have failed some part of the course: such students may still be able to get some kind of qualification, and the viva will probably include an attempt to find out more about the capabilities of the student – in the areas where he or she has some ability. Inevitably, it will also focus on the problem area and how it relates to the rest of the course.

3. Any student whose results show a wide variation in grades: it would be unusual for a student who, for example, obtained over 70 per cent on some papers to get only 50 per cent on others. If the discrepancy has no obvious reason, the student might be asked to attend a viva to find out whether the low mark had some cause which might suggest a generous response. The student is given the opportunity to show whether there is real competence in the subject with the low grade, or whether perhaps there really is less understanding or less effort to understand. The low mark will not be reduced as a result of the viva, but it might be improved.

4. Borderline students: students who are on the borderline between two grades or classes of result may be given a viva to allow them the possibility of getting the higher grade. In a way, this is a matter of standards between institutions: marking, however careful and however often checked, still has a subjective element, and it would be a pity if a student were to get a lower result because of harsher marking than might have been received elsewhere. Such a viva, probably the most commonly held, is always in terms of the student getting a better grade, never in order to reduce the result.

5. Students with particular problems: sometimes a department will ask for a viva for a student who has a difficulty or disability which might have affected the result – dyslexia might be an example. The viva is principally requested as support for the department, which wants to be absolutely sure that such students have been fairly treated and not penalised in any way for reasons beyond their control.

6. Suspicion of plagiarism: this is a sad form of viva, but sometimes necessary when examiners suspect that students have produced work that is not their own. I stressed earlier in this book (page 31) the need to respect intellectual property and the serious nature of any breach of this respect; students who appear to have cheated in this way will be given a viva and asked to explain their work in their own words, in order to show whether there is real understanding or not. At this stage, they will have to prove that they did not cheat, rather than have their innocence assumed.

I have described the major reasons for vivas, but there are occasionally others, such as a number of randomly chosen students being called for viva in order to check the overall standard (in which case, the student might benefit from the viva but would certainly not lose by it), or, especially in the case of advanced or postgraduate courses, because of the interest of the external examiner, who might wish to discuss further work or publication.

Whatever the reason for the viva, we have seen that it takes place in order to help the student and not as a punishment. It is a sad fact that students tend to have a very different idea of a viva, and feel that there is some sort of disgrace in being asked to attend. Inevitably, this makes them even more nervous than usual, which may prevent them from showing themselves at their best. Except perhaps for the 'plagiarism' occasion, a viva is an opportunity for the student and should be viewed as such. Indeed, part of the value of a viva might be to encourage a very good student to think in terms of further work or research.

In order for a viva to take place, there must be examiners present. The number and status of these varies widely, but there will usually be more than one, and often three. They will probably include at least one member of staff who has taught the student and at least one external examiner, who will have come from another institution to ensure that appropriate standards are kept and that each student is treated fairly. In courses which are validated by an outside non-academic body, such as an engineering institution, there may also be an industrial representative acting as an additional external examiner.

If you are called for a viva, the presence of people who are unknown to you will have some impact on your preparation and thinking. It is in a sense an interview, and it would be sensible therefore to take some care with your appearance and dress; while I wouldn't want to overstress this, an examiner who has never seen you before will inevitably react well if you have clearly made an effort to look reasonably professional – it is in any case a compliment to the people present.

While your tutor will be familiar with the work that you have done, an external examiner won't be; this should be kept in mind, so that you explain why a particular line was followed rather than taking it for granted that everybody knows. If there is also an industrialist present, it's likely that questions from that source will have a more practical, industry-related direction than questions from other people; 'In your job, how would you handle such a problem?'; 'What do you think could be the practical applications of such a development?', and so on. It would be a good idea, in such cases, to think in advance about the practical ramifications of your last year's project or your dissertation subject.

This isn't the only way in which you need to prepare for a viva. Its importance is obvious, but each year some students either miss an announcement that the viva will take place, or fail to turn up at the right time and place. Check that you are not going to miss the opportunity of benefiting from your viva. If you are called to attend, take time the night before to think about likely areas of questioning; read through your dissertation again to remind yourself of the work you did and the decisions you had to make; think about the course in terms of what you specialised in, your particular interests, or any work you would like to develop further.

There are some things in common between a formal presentation (see page 139), a viva and a job interview (see page 187). You are nervous in a similar way, and you can use your nerves to help you to appear alert and to think quickly. Smile at your examiners when you greet them, respond if they offer to shake hands, sit down only when you are asked to do so – and then sit well back in the chair so that you can be as comfortable as possible, at the same time looking professional. Make eye contact with each questioner, and if you need to, take time to answer. It's much better to pause and think first than to rush in with a response and regret it a minute later.

You may be asked to draw a quick sketch or a simple graph in answer to a question. Drawing on a blackboard isn't easy, and you may prefer to draw on a piece of paper; if you do this, take your time, draw your sketch from your point of view, and then turn it round to show the panel. This is much safer than trying to draw upside down as if from their point of view, while explaining what you are doing at the same time.

At the end of the viva, thank the examiners with a smile, and walk out confidently. Remember that you will not have lost anything by the occasion, and you may well have gained.

There is one extra interview which an external examiner may request, which is in no way assessed and which gives you the chance to discuss how you felt about your subject and the way in which it has been handled. Occasionally, an examiner might ask the department to choose a cross-section of students and to allow a short group discussion about the composition of the course. This happens most often if the course is externally validated by a professional body. You will naturally not be asked to comment on any particular lecturer, but you might be asked how new subjects have fitted in with the rest of the course, what the balance of the course is between different aspects, and perhaps about your own aspirations for the future. This is useful information which can be discussed later (totally anonymously as far as you are concerned) and perhaps taken back for discussion by the validating body. It is not a common occurrence, but it is a chance to influence, in a small way, the lives and work of future students.

▶ Project interviews (project vivas)

At the end of a major project, you may be asked to discuss your work on an individual basis even if the project itself has been undertaken in a group. In this case, all students are likely to have vivas, not just those in the categories I mentioned earlier. There may be two or three examiners, all of whom may be known to you; one is likely to have the role of moderator, to ensure that the level of questioning remains more or less constant. All are likely to have read your report, which means that it's essential that you have reread it recently, so that it's fresh in your mind. It may be appropriate for you to take a copy of your report and your project logbook with you to the interview.

Such an interview is designed to assess various aspects of your work; in this section, we have used a student engineering design project as an example, but the range of questions is likely to be similar whatever your specialism. If you are given a few minutes at the start to describe what you have done, give a short, structured introduction (which you have planned in advance), without rambling from the subject or going into too much detail. You are then likely to be asked questions from the following categories.

1. *Professionalism*: how professional has your approach been? Have you used your theoretical knowledge and applied it in a sensible way? Have you observed safety rules? What has been your approach to the design: have you sufficiently considered alternatives, compromised when this is appropriate, considered the cost/weight implications of your design, made sensible choices? What aptitude have you shown in the practical manufacture and testing stages?

   Obviously, in a short interview it will be impossible to assess all these considerations, but the examiners will have some prior knowledge of what you have done, and will select their questions accordingly.

2. *Technical issues*: these questions will be very specific to your project; you are likely to be asked why you made certain decisions, whether your checking and testing were thorough, how far you have really understood the technical details of the work and whether you are aware of its possible applications. If you have carried out the project in collaboration with another student, it is essential that you can show understanding of the whole project, not just the parts for which you were responsible.

3. *Effective communication of your work*: this part of the interview will be based on your report. Sadly, it is possible for students to have an almost complete lack of understanding of what they have written. Your examiners may pick up on quite minor details of your report, and you must be familiar with your work so that you can plan your answer quickly. Check back in advance what your main sources were for your reading and research, and be prepared to refer to them. A common problem nowadays is for students to take information wholesale from the Internet without any reference; as such information is ephemeral, they are then unable to find it again, and as time passes, the information becomes less and less clear to them, so that by the time they are asked about it, it seems totally unfamiliar. (The use of such sources was discussed in an earlier chapter, page 35.)

   The quality of your writing may now be under scrutiny. If it is ungrammatical, badly punctuated or otherwise unchecked (see page 89), you may be asked to read it aloud and then to explain it. Needless to say, the best students have checked their work thoroughly before handing it in, and read it through again thoughtfully, shortly before the interview.

4. *Management issues*: the project itself has, among other things, been a test of your management potential. You may be asked about your time management, how you allocated time and divided the work between you. You could also be asked about group working – how well did you and your partner work together? – and the issues connected with group working which you are now aware of, such as mutual support and fair division of labour. Your interaction with colleagues, technicians and other support staff, and your commitment to the work, might be discussed. These are issues which will become very important to you in your job, and it's right that they should play a part in your preparation for the future.

Your interview is unlikely to last more than half an hour, and it may be shorter than that; there will not be time to ask you about all these aspects of your work, and on the whole, once they have tried to put you at your ease, examiners will look for perceived weaknesses and question you about them. The more time you can give to preparation before the interview, the less likely you are to find the questions difficult or the situation overwhelmingly stressful.

There is one further point about stress which should be noticed, and which perhaps applies more in a project interview than in other forms of viva. Your project work has occupied much of your time for several months, perhaps the whole year, and in some ways it's very close to your heart (even if you didn't greatly enjoy it). If you are then feeling very tense about the interview, you may react in one of two undesirable ways: you may try to pass off any weaknesses as the responsibility of your partner(s), or you may respond to questions in an aggressive way.

Neither response will do you credit, even if the examiners recognise that it is the result of stress rather than ill will. Try to look and sound enthusiastic about your work, and see it as a chance to talk about something which you enjoyed, to people who want to hear what you have to say. You will sometimes be in a comparable situation at work, and if you see it as a positive and challenging opportunity, you can achieve a sympathetic and supportive audience even if everything hasn't worked out quite as well as you'd hoped.

▶ Project colloquia

A project colloquium is very similar to a formal presentation (see page 131), but as it sometimes forms part of a final examination, it is worth commenting briefly about it now. The form will vary, but we have taken as an example the colloquia held each year in a department of computer science.

The colloquium follows the completion of the final year project; all students have to make a short presentation on the subject of their project before an audience which consists of two members of staff, both of whom have had no prior links with the project, and fellow final year students who will themselves be taking part in the colloquium. Each student is allocated ten minutes to present the topic, with a cut-off time of twelve minutes after which the presentation will be stopped (for the importance of accurate timing and how to achieve it, see page 120). The presentation is followed by five minutes of questions from the audience.

Students are encouraged to use visual aids (see page 122), and are allowed to use material, suitably adapted, from their final project report. As the aim is to assess the students' effectiveness in communicating their work and their ideas, they are expected to hold the audience's interest and to show their own enthusiasm.

The mark sheet has six sections, each of which is given a grade, as shown below.

Possible mark sheet for a project colloquium

- Visual material: quality and effectiveness of visual aids
- Oral presentation: must be clear and succinct
- Technical content: must be appropriately chosen and technically accurate
- Timing: time management must be in keeping with the rules
- Presentation style: should be lively, interesting, and positive
- Questions: how did the student handle and answer questions from the audience?

This is one example of a presentation which is assessed as part of a final examination, but many courses include a similar occasion. Elsewhere in this book there is detailed help with aspects of a successful presentation such as handling notes, timing, and building an effective rapport with the audience (see Chapters 6 and 7).

▶ Poster presentations

Poster presentations are particularly popular in pure science departments, and also at conferences in the same subjects. Students are asked to research and prepare information about a topic in poster form; the audience then walks round the posters and at each is given a short presentation about the subject, with the poster used as a visual aid. This is a comparatively informal kind of presentation, and the numbers in the audience at any one time will be small, not least because of the difficulty of displaying a poster to many people at the same time. Sometimes there will be no actual presentation, but questions from the group looking at the poster, and an informal discussion.

Posters may be A0 size, or a little smaller. Make sure that every detail can be clearly seen, and read, by people who may be standing a metre away; this will restrict the amount you can show (see also visual aids, page 124). Nowadays, posters are often professionally printed on a single sheet and laminated; you may be able to have your poster produced comparatively cheaply within your institution, perhaps in the library. You will then be able to transport it quite easily, rolled up in a tube.

Plan what you want to say, as with any other presentation. Even if you are simply answering questions, try to foresee what people will ask, and think how you can briefly and clearly explain your work. Try to avoid long explanations – your audience is with you only for a short time, and will want to move on to other posters.

▶ Computer demonstrations

Students of computer science may be asked to take part in types of presentation which are less common in other subjects. In this book, it is not possible to discuss at length every form of oral examination which might have a place in academic life, but as work with computers becomes more widely integrated into other fields of study, students may be called on to demonstrate their work by similar means.

A computer demonstration, probably lasting for about ten minutes, requires students to present their projects to a small audience, perhaps two or three members of staff who have not been involved in the project itself. This requires very careful preparation. As always, the first stage is to decide on the objectives: as the main motive will be to convince the audience that the project was well researched and developed, students will need to decide what particular features will best demonstrate this. The biggest danger is of overwhelming with detail; computers can show a great deal of information very rapidly, and there is inevitably a temptation to present as much material as possible in the time available, which is not sensible and will not be effective.

If students clarify to themselves exactly what they should present, they then have a basis for pruning the images to those which demonstrate the key message. What is shown must reveal the technical achievement of the project, and a decision must be made about the appropriate technical depth which can be shown in a limited time. It is easy to assume that the product itself, its functionality, user-friendliness, innovative features and reliability, is all that is being assessed; these features are of course essential, but an examiner is also considering the presentation itself, the quality of the general overview which must precede the details, the pace, clarity and style with which the material is presented.

Needless to say, this demands thorough rehearsal, not least so that students can ensure that their program is ready when the examiners arrive. Some aspects of a good presentation, such as eye contact, are difficult if the presenter is watching the screen, but at least at the beginning and end of the presentation, and sometimes in answering a question, there is an opportunity to face the audience. The pace of the demonstration is especially important: neither the images nor the voice should give an impression of speed or overanxiety.

▶ The walk-through

The 'walk-through' is a form of discussion/negotiation which is used in the computer software industry and has found its way into some academic courses. It is certainly useful that students who are likely to meet the process at work have some practice beforehand, and it is also a good introduction to negotiation skills.

As part of the design activity, groups of students present to one another ('expose to' is the usual expression) their work so far, and ask for advice and comments, not solutions. The intention is to reveal any defects in the thinking, to suggest alternative approaches or to put forward any other ideas which might benefit the group's work. The occasion must not become competitive or confrontational.

There are difficulties for both the presenting group and the responding ('auditing') group. The former group is responsible for setting the scene, and presenting enough of a context to make questions and comments feasible. They have to be selective – it would not be sensible to spend time going through the whole of the project – and at the same time open in what they say. They must avoid 'selling' or self-congratulation; instead, they must present their ideas in a way which allows for criticism – and they must not be defensive or aggressive when it comes. It is a difficult role, and the introductory material must be thought through with great care. The group members also have to trust one another, so that no one tries either to hide behind others or to take over the group (for a further discussion of group presentations, see Chapter 5).

However, the presenting group at least has the chance to prepare; the auditing group has to think and respond quickly, on the basis of perhaps a short paper about the subject given in advance by the presenters, but principally on the information which they are given at the start of the walk-through. They have to be able to think of perceptive questions and comments at very short notice, and to put their thoughts across in a way which is acceptable to the other students. Inevitably, tensions and rivalries sometimes arise, but all comments must be offered in a non-destructive way ('Have you considered a different approach?' rather than 'I think you're going about this in the wrong way.').

The assessment of such an occasion is very difficult, and must be made on a group basis, by more than one member of staff. Nevertheless, the walk-through experience is valuable in helping students to understand that, in an organisation, people need to be able to work together even when their views differ, and that it's sometimes necessary to admit difficulties and accept advice in order to be successful – both useful skills to have learnt during the education process.

▶ **Key points**

▶ Vivas are generally intended to help you, so adopt a positive frame of mind; check the details and arrive in plenty of time

▶ Prepare for your viva by rereading your final project report or dissertation, and reminding yourself of work you completed during your course

▶ Treat the viva as a kind of interview, and respond as thoughtfully and accurately as you can, making eye contact with the examiners and taking your time over difficult answers

▶ If you have a final project interview, assess the practical implications or applications of your work, the decisions you had to make, and the technical issues involved. Sound enthusiastic about your work

▶ A project colloquium or poster presentation may be part of your final exam. Check the exact form this will take, and prepare carefully, reminding yourself of your presentation skills

▶ The timing of a computer demonstration is very important. Ensure that your program is ready when the examiner arrives, and don't try to rush through information on the screen

▶ In a walk-through, you will have to present prepared ideas and also respond to information prepared by other people. Be ready to listen, question courteously and adopt a flexible approach to new and perhaps challenging material

Part Four
Applying for a Job

9 Preparing a CV and Job Application

Some people arrive at college or university already knowing what their future careers are likely to be: if you take a medical degree, you are likely to become a doctor, nurse or similar medical professional; if you study accountancy, you are likely to look for work as an accountant. However, you may move away from hands-on science or engineering into teaching, personnel or management; by the time you finish, you may have come across areas of work which you had never heard of when your course began.

You will probably ask for and receive advice in deciding how to choose a career, from your tutor, professional people whom you know through vacation jobs or family links or leisure activities, and, especially, your Careers Advisory Service. It is wise to make contact with careers specialists early on in your study; if you are taking a three-year course, certainly by the middle of your second year. These advisors have detailed information about possible careers, and can help you to assess yourself so that you have a clearer idea of what you are, and are not, suited to. They will also, of course, have information about vacancies, especially in local organisations.

In this section, I shan't attempt to discuss career choice, personality and aptitude tests, or the many ways to find a job; you will have access to plenty of help in these areas. I shall concentrate instead on the communication aspects of applying for jobs: in this chapter, completing application forms, preparing a CV, and writing a covering letter; in the next chapter, using communication skills successfully during job interviews.

As with so many aspects of writing and speaking, preparation is essential. It is worth looking at job adverts in appropriate journals, newspapers and, nowadays, on the Internet, before you actually need to respond to them. Get a feeling for the way in which they are worded, and for the information they request – and the form in which they want it – so that you start to recognise common patterns. At your Careers

Advisory Service, look at application forms to see how they are presented and the information they typically require, and think how you would respond if you wanted to apply for the job. In this way, when the appropriate time comes, you will be prepared to face the long process of job hunting, and you are unlikely to be daunted by a long and apparently fearsome application form.

▶ Application forms

Company forms can be unnerving at first sight: you are restricted in the amount that you can write, and yet they seem to ask far-reaching questions about you, your abilities and your interests. I'll discuss a typical form in three sections, the first being a comparatively simple request for identification – your name, address, date of birth, and so on. The second is likely to be a section about your academic background, examination results and work experience. Finally, and much the hardest to complete, there is the small section which contains what look like the trick questions, about why you want the job and why you feel that you are suited to this type of career.

Preliminary work
It is very tempting to complete the first section of your form straightaway, as it appears to present no difficulties. Resist this temptation. Before you fill in any part of the form, photocopy it, and complete the photocopy first, putting the form itself carefully away in a folder until you are ready to handle it. Using a photocopy not only allows you to ensure that what you want to say fits the space allocated, it also gives you the chance to have your writing checked while you can still have a second or third attempt if you need it. Furthermore, you will have a record of what you put on the form so that you can look at it again before you go to an interview.

Your photocopy should now be completed in the same way as your final version, which means that you must decide whether to handwrite the form or try to complete it on the computer. I use the word 'try' advisedly: it is extremely difficult to ensure that typed text fits exactly into the boxes provided, and the effort is probably not worthwhile. Unless you are expressly asked not to do so, complete your form by hand and in black ink – it will be photocopied by the company that receives it, and black ink gives a clearer image than any other colour (it is in any case seen as eccentric to use any colour apart from black and blue; you want to make your mark, but not to be regarded as odd).

However, I did say 'unless ... ', and this is an important proviso: before completing any job application, on a form or in any other way, always check that you are doing what the advertisement asks for; the person responsible for the first sifting of responses will almost certainly throw away any application which has not followed the style requested.

Before you start work, make sure that you note in your diary the date by which you need to have the form completed and sent off. Always allow at least three days before the deadline, as the post can let you down or a weekend can get in the way; if your form arrives late, you will not get the job, however good your results.

This is also the time to contact your referees. You will already know of two or three people who have agreed to provide references for you, and at this stage you need to decide which are the most appropriate for this particular application. Your personal tutor, course tutor or head of department will almost certainly be a regular referee, and you may also have a particular reason for choosing your second – your manager from a vacation job in the same industry, for instance. Unless you have 'global' permission to use someone's name whenever you apply for a job, always ask before filling in the name and address, and let your referees know the type of job you have applied for, and any particular points that they may not be aware of, for instance, that you have worked temporarily in a similar position and therefore have experience. It is discourteous not to ask, as writing references is a considerable, and time-consuming, responsibility, and it is sensible to make sure that your referees have all the appropriate information so that they can do their best to support your application.

Facts and figures

You are now ready to complete the first part of your practice form. It seems easy, but there are dangers even at this stage. Make sure that you give your name in its official form: everyone may know you as Susie, but you are Susan on the form (unless, of course, your birth certificate refers to you as 'Susie'). It goes without saying that you must use your legal name, even if you normally use a different one (for instance, that of a step-parent), not least so that it's consistent with your certificates. Give your date of birth in a clear, unambiguous way: day, followed by month written as a word, and then year. You will also probably have to give your nationality and two addresses, one for term time and one for vacations.

Your term address is presumably obvious, but think about your home address. If you have two 'home' addresses, consider where you are most likely to be during the next vacation, and how quickly post could be forwarded to you if necessary. The same applies to telephone numbers (include the codes); if you have a term-time e-mail address, then give that as well, if space permits. Trying out your information on a photocopy of the form helps you to check how much you can write in the boxes: a long postal address may have to be written in small letters if the space is limited.

Other personal information may be needed, for instance your next of kin; this is not necessarily your nearest living relative, but the person who can most easily be contacted if you should have an accident or become seriously ill. You may also be asked whether you are married or not, and whether you are related to anyone in the organisation. Be honest about this: if you know about the job because your favourite aunt is one of their research scientists, it will do you no harm to say so, and in any case it would be difficult to keep the relationship secret if you ended up working in the same laboratory.

Other questions in this section may be about mobility – are you willing to work anywhere in the country? – and your availability for interview (if this is not mentioned, include it in your covering letter). Give yourself as much flexibility as possible in answering both these questions: if you are willing and able to live in a new area, you will increase your chances of being employed; if you are available most of the time for an interview, this is obviously helpful but remember to exclude the time when you will be sitting your examinations!

Education, work and leisure

The next section of your form is likely to be about your educational achievements. This is one of the places where space gives you a clue about how much to include. If you passed four A levels and ten GCSEs, but the space provided precludes your listing all these successes, it seems reasonable to assume that a prospective employer is more inter-ested in A levels than in anything earlier, and you might just summarise ('10 GCSEs, including 6 A grades'). Some people have the additional problem of having moved around during their childhood, often because of a parent's job; the result is a list of schools attended which is too long for the space. If this happens, cut out the earliest schools, and start with those at which you took your principal exami-nations, such as NVQs, GCSEs and A levels.

If you still have to take your final examinations, say so, and estimate your likely class of result if you are asked to do so (having checked with your tutor first – there's no point in either under- or overestimating your results). You may also be asked about any prizes you have won, or any advanced course (postgraduate courses, for example); if you haven't done any of these things, just leave the section empty. The chances are that most other applicants won't have anything to report here, either.

Above all, tell the truth. We have all heard grisly stories of people who cheated (because that's what it is) by pretending to outstanding results which they didn't get, and whose behaviour was found out because the company asked to see the certificate (they often do), or the reference made the truth clear, or they simply met someone from their past life at the wrong moment. The reality of the situation is often discovered, and even if you get away with it, you have to live with the risk of being found out, or with the problem of trying to do a job for which you really aren't qualified. The opposite problem is much rarer, but occasionally people hide an extra qualification in case they seem to be overqualified for a particular job. They can still be dismissed for dishonest behaviour in omitting relevant information; in applications, as in most things, honesty is much the best policy.

You will almost certainly be asked about your work experience, which may relate to a year out, or to part-time or vacation work. The importance of this is often underestimated. Include as much information as you can, and think through the experience and what you gained from it: you may be asked on the form ('Which parts of this experience were most beneficial to you, and why?'), and you may have to give further details at the interview stage. It's tempting to think that spending three evenings a week working behind a bar is not much help if you are applying for a job as a software developer, but you would be wrong. You have worked as part of a small team in a restricted space and often under pressure; you have had to communicate with a range of people and to keep cool if there are signs of trouble; you have had to think quickly, and to look and sound friendly even if you were very tired or fed up; you have had to prove yourself to be reliable. All these are highly desirable characteristics from the employer's point of view, and you may well be able to draw attention to them at the appropriate point of the form (if not, remember the interview).

If your work experience has been valuable, so too has your leisure time. Employers are interested in your outside interests because they want to know not just that you can do the job but also that you will fit into the organisation, and that you will be pleasant to work with. Think through your interests carefully, and if necessary, select the most suitable. If you have too many interests, you may give the impression that you don't have much time for work; if you have only reading and watching films, you will come across as rather dull and isolated. Most work in industry is carried out by teams rather than by individuals, and taking part in group activities such as team sports or amateur dramatics shows that you are used to and enjoy working with other people. Ideally, you will present a mixture of interests, some involving other people, some quieter and more thoughtful.

Have you held positions of responsibility in any of your leisure activities? If so, these too may say something useful about you: if you were the treasurer of a society, people must have trusted you, and you will have gained some financial awareness; if you organised a major social event, you probably have good managerial abilities, including the very valuable ability to motivate people; if you are president of the rock climbing club, you may well be a risk-taker but you may also be ready to take responsibility for other people's safety and wellbeing.

Don't waste this valuable experience, but at the same time, take care that whatever you say fits sensibly into the space provided. Filling in an application form efficiently says something about your ability to get essential information across clearly and concisely, and that in itself is an important message.

As with exam results, tell the truth also about your hobbies. You may be asked about them at your interview, and if you clearly know very little about mountaineering in spite of claiming it as one of your interests, you will give a poor impression and could be caught out. How were you to know that one of the panel at your interview spends all his holidays in the Alps?

Two questions probably remain in this section of the form: health and additional skills. The former must be handled in a straightforward, truthful way (you may have to have a medical later). There are laws against discriminating against people with disabilities, but in any case it is unwise to hide any health problems in case they cause difficulty at work later on. Many people suffer from asthma, and if you do, you would not want to be sent to work in a dusty environment.

People often undersell themselves in the 'additional information' section. Any familiarity with computers and software packages is likely to be useful – there are few jobs nowadays in which computer literacy is not an advantage. Are you familiar with any foreign languages? Even if your knowledge is limited, it is worth saying that you have a little French, Spanish or other language; it might be very useful in greeting overseas clients, even if the conversation has to switch to English. Do you have a clean driving licence? Even if you are not going to have a company car straightaway, being able to drive is always an advantage. Have you taken first aid qualifications? Any of these skills might just put you ahead of the competition, and so might win you an interview.

What made you choose ... ?

The final section of the form is much the most difficult to complete. It consists essentially of two questions: why are you choosing this career, and why are you suited to this job? The wording will vary, but this is what they want to know, and much weight may be put on the way in which you respond.

So far, you have written single words, short phrases or brief sentences; at this point you will be writing perhaps a longish paragraph, half a page or even a full page, and your information is much less structured. Why have you chosen this particular career, and why do you think you are suited to it? Think back to your schooldays. What made you apply for the course you have been taking? Has your perception of possible careers changed since then? Have you made choices during your course, about which area of the subject to concentrate on? Which part of your course have you enjoyed most, and why? These are only pointers, and you will want to support them by talking again to your careers counsellor, or taking an aptitude test. Don't rush this part of the form: you need to make the link between the career you want to embark on and your own particular abilities, likes and dislikes.

This will lead you naturally to consider the job itself. Think about what you know of the work for which you are applying. Are you likely to be part of a team, to travel, to work mainly with people? Is the organisation large enough to offer you career choices when you are already employed, or small enough to be creating a niche for itself, to be looking for ways of establishing itself among the market leaders? Are you looking for excellent laboratory facilities in order to develop your own research potential while you are working; do you prefer computer software to hardware; is the company involved with a particular project which has appealed to you; have you tried a similar job during the vacation and found it both challenging and rewarding?

This is the kind of consideration which will help you to answer these questions. Be careful not to go 'over the top'; comments about how wonderful the company is will put off the reader because they sound false and often patronising. Be honest about the appeal of this type of work, what you feel you would like to get out of it and what you have to offer, and write your answer simply, clearly and concisely.

Checking and completing the form

When your photocopy of the form is complete, check it. Look up any words you are unsure of in the dictionary; ask someone else's advice about punctuation or grammar if you are unsure, and ask one or two friends to read the whole form through to see if you have left out anything important or been unclear at any point.

You are now ready to fill in the form itself. Try to do so at a desk or table, with a good light, no interruptions, and plenty of time. At this stage, you don't want to make a mistake, but if you do, use tippex as sparingly as possible, and remember to write in the correct letters when the space is dry. Fold the form as it was (or was not) folded when it reached you, and address it as indicated in the advertisement. Add your covering letter (see page 17), and send off the whole application. Finally, file your last photocopied version, as you may need to look at it again later, if you are called for an interview.

▶ The curriculum vitae

Some companies favour application forms, and others prefer a curriculum vitae (CV), that is, the story of your life. Generally, this means that you will give more or less the same information, but the format will be up to you; as a result, you will have much less guidance about the amount of detail needed – there will be no small box to complete. The layout will be your choice, although there are conventions which should be followed, and the length is again a matter for you to decide. At the stage you are likely to have reached, you are almost certain to need more than one page for your CV; at the same time, you don't want it to get out of hand, reaching five or six pages in length – two pages is about the norm at this point of your career. Most of all, you want to make the right impact, which means that you must draw attention to what your readers will want to know.

All this sounds daunting, but it won't be, if you decide on a simple but clear format. One of the advantages of a CV is that you can produce it on a word processor, with the help of a spellcheck and the ability to correct mistakes quickly and easily. You may even ask someone else to type up your CV for you, and, if you are not good at the effective layout of information, this has much to recommend it. I'm not, however, suggesting that you spend a great deal of money answering an advertisement offering to 'prepare a perfect CV for you'; you know more about you than anyone else does, and you should think through your CV for yourself; a little help with the typing is a different matter. One other catch is worth mentioning: if you use someone else's CV as your template, simply putting your own information where a friend's was originally, remember to check that you have changed all the details. I heard of a case in which the original date of birth was accidentally left in place; unfortunately, the original writer was three years older, and the producer of the new CV thus had three unexplained years!

CV format

Usually, CVs, like application forms, fall into three sections. First, there is the general identifying information, such as name, date of birth, addresses for term time and vacation, and so on. This is usually set out with headings in bold type to the left, and the detailed information to the right (see example, page 175). The same principles apply as with forms: use legally accepted names, write your date of birth unambiguously, think about the addresses and telephone numbers you give (see page 163). As long as all the appropriate information is given, this section is not difficult, and of course you can easily correct any mistakes or change your mind about the layout.

The first major difference in the two forms of application comes with the section about your education. The bold heading will again appear at the left, but the order of information may well be different. You are still on the first page of your document, and you want to draw the reader's attention to the most important details. These will not be the GCSEs you obtained several years ago, but your most recent qualification (or the qualification you hope to obtain when the results are known). This must therefore come first, with the additional information needed by the reader, that is, if you are at a university, your degree result (or predicted result), and the university you attended, with dates.

You now have the opportunity to embellish this basic information. Your prospective employer will be interested to know which special subjects or options you took, and the title of your final year project or dissertation. These details show your particular areas of interest, and perhaps also of ability; this may be crucial if you are applying to work in a highly specialised area of the company. You may find that you take one or two paragraphs to explain all this, but it is much more important to the reader than the earlier detail, which you may summarise if you wish (see page 164).

Using appropriate headings with dates, as in the example, you can now work backwards through your schooling, including your final school examination results, but probably not much detail before that. In each case, give the name of the school you attended, the dates of your examination successes, and the grades you obtained. This information may not be of great interest to the reader, but it shows your range of study; your results in English Language and Mathematics tend to be most useful in showing your basic educational level in two very important areas, and languages, for instance, are often useful even at an elementary level.

When you have dealt with your education, you can start a new heading, Work Experience. Again, start with the most recent, using the dates of your employment as left-hand headings and the name of your employer as a heading to the right (see example, page 176). Under this, give a short account of your responsibilities and any aspects of the job which seem particularly relevant to the post for which you are applying. Interpret this quite widely, bearing in mind the value of even the most humble of jobs (see comments above, page 165). You may write a paragraph or even two paragraphs about your most recent experience, and perhaps rather less about earlier work; list details as bullet points if it seems appropriate, but if you do this, make sure that your list has a brief introduction and is consistent in style (see section about the layout of lists in Chapter 3, page 49).

Your next heading is likely to be Other Relevant Experience. As with the application form, this is where you give details of languages, computer literacy, driving licence and so on. Include any sort of qualification which an employer might find useful, first aid certificates, for example. You are drawing attention to the qualities which make you stand out from other candidates.

This is also true of Outside Interests, which will probably be your final heading. Suggestions have been given in the section on application forms (see page 165), but in a CV you have the space to say a little about these interests, especially any positions of responsibility which you held. Don't waffle, though; this section should not become too long.

Finally, you will add the names and addresses of your referees. Give two, unless you are told otherwise in the advertisement, one being from your current educational institution and the other from your work experience, or someone who has known you well for at least a couple of years. If you are likely to apply for a number of jobs, you may want to have two or three 'other' referees, so that one person doesn't have to spend too much time writing about you; you will always need the reference from your university or college, but it is part of your tutor's job, and so there should be no problem about using the same name several times. Always let your referees know anything which they might need to include, for instance extra qualifications which they might not know about.

Much of the information included in a CV is similar to that asked for in an application form, but there is no obvious place in the CV for the 'why do you want this career/job?' section. You will therefore need to include it in your covering letter.

However, before you start work on the letter, you need to go through the same final checking of your CV as you would with the form: is everything clear, accurate, complete, with the extra dimension, is the layout attractive and easy to follow? Your CV will probably be about two pages long; try not to let it grow to more than three pages, unless you are a mature student with a wealth of previous work experience. (There is a specimen CV on page 175.)

▶ The covering letter

Every application form or CV should be sent with a covering letter. This is partly a matter of courtesy, partly in order to help the company to which you are applying, and partly to give you a final opportunity to show that you are worth interviewing.

Every letter has a conventional format, although in practice we often abbreviate this in an informal situation, for instance, in writing to a friend we may not bother with our own address in detail, because the friend already knows it well. The covering letter for an application is just about the most formal letter we ever write, and so every detail must be given fully and accurately.

Before you start, look again at the advertisement to check whether you have been given any guidance about the form your letter should take, for instance, whether it should be hand or computer written. If it is up to you, you really do have a choice: handwriting may seem more immediate and personal, and a word processed letter more formal and professional. Either way, it must be well presented and carefully checked for possible errors either of style or of writing.

The basic format for a letter includes your own address (not your name) at the top right-hand corner of the page, followed by the date, and the recipient's name and address at the left-hand side, usually positioned so that it starts a line lower than the date. An example is given later in this chapter (see page 178). Give the addresses in full, including the postcode, and write the date in a modern, unambiguous way (9 May 1999 is a common and acceptable form).

At the head of the recipient's address, you will need a name. Usually, this is given in the advertisement; check that you give it in exactly the same form. If for some reason you don't have a name, for instance if the advertisement simply says to 'The Personnel Manager', you have two possibilities. You can address the letter in this way, in which case you are limited to the very awkward 'Dear Sir or Madam' at the beginning of the text, or you can ring up the company and ask the person on the switchboard for the name of the personnel manager. If there is any doubt, ask to be put through to the personnel department, explain that you wish to apply for the job, and ask for the name. You are unlikely to find yourself speaking to the personnel manager, but if by any chance you do, what happens? You explain, and the manager gives you the information. You are already making a good impression as someone who pays attention to detail, and who will take time and trouble in order to get the job.

If you do this, you will be able to address your letter appropriately, which helps you as you begin to write. When you start with the name of the individual, you can also finish the letter with 'Yours sincerely' (capital Y, small s), which sounds more friendly than the ending 'Yours faithfully' (capital Y, small f) which by convention has to follow an introduction with no personal name, that is, 'Dear Sir or Madam' or similar. These conventions are very strong, and you are well advised to follow them in such an important letter.

After the greeting, give your letter a heading. This may be 'Your ref: ... ' or the name of the post you are applying for, set out on a line by itself and in bold type, so that it acts in the same way as a heading in a report.

I said above that a covering letter is of help to the company. Advertising vacancies is an expensive operation, and it is always useful to know which advertisement was the most productive in terms of response. At the beginning of your letter, therefore, you need to let the recipient know how you found out about the job. First, identify the post you are applying for, if your heading hasn't already done this, so that if the company is advertising for a range of new employees, there is no confusion about the post you have in mind. Then say where you saw the advertisement, including the name of the newspaper or journal, and the date of the specific issue. If you found out about the job in some different way, for instance through your Careers Office, then say so. All this is of help to the company, and it also enables you to start writing the letter in a straightforward, objective way.

You now have a small amount of space (a covering letter should not be more than one page in length) in which to draw the reader's attention to the most important features of your form or CV; tell them as briefly and effectively as you can why you want this particular job, and why you feel that you are well suited to it.

This section needs careful planning. Think in terms of four bullet points – you could write the middle of your letter in this form if you feel it is helpful – which explain your abilities and interests as clearly as possible. Look carefully at the original advertisement, and try to identify exactly what they are looking for. Do they ask for a good communicator? You might want to quote a particularly high mark which you obtained at your project presentation. Do they ask for someone to be part of a team? Remember that your project was a joint one, three of you working together, and so you have some experience of teamwork. Does the advertisement state that you would be working with customers? You met the public when you took a vacation job in a local department store. Are you likely to travel as part of the job? You took a foreign language at A level, and spent a long vacation travelling in the Far East. Dissect the advertisement and any other information you have been able to find about the company, for instance through its website, to form the clearest possible picture of the kind of person they are looking for. When you have done that, match yourself to this picture as exactly as the truth will allow; choose four points which seem to you to be of particular importance, and list them in the middle of your letter. Remember that a list needs to be introduced, and use something like 'Your advertisement asks for ability in communication and in relating to customers. These are areas in which I feel that I have particular skills and interest, as can be seen from my previous work:' and follow this with your four bullet points.

After this, you will have very little space left. Indicate when you could be available for interview, giving as much scope as possible, and when, if you were appointed, you could start work. Be realistic about this, as it may be better to allow for a short holiday than to start work and then realise that you haven't had a break since you finished your exams; at the same time, don't delay the start date for too long, or the prospective employer may look for someone else who could begin more quickly. Your letter will need what is generally called a 'courtesy close' sentence such as 'I look forward to hearing from you', and then you can sign off in the appropriate form, depending on how you began the letter. Your signature must stand by itself, with no title (Mr and so on) attached to it, but you should also print your name underneath, so that it can be easily identified.

As before, ask a friend to check that you have written clearly and accurately; you would be well advised to photocopy both CV and letter, so that you have a good version for later use if necessary (see the following section). Use an envelope of the same colour as the paper, address it exactly according to the advertisement, and send it first class, as you want to show that you are keenly interested in the job.

▶ Online applications

An increasing number of companies have their own websites, which often carry information about their particular requirements and their current vacancies. This is obviously a good and up-to-date way of finding out about jobs, and you may be able to order further information or a brochure online. You may find an application form which you can use via the Internet; you may also be able to e-mail your application.

Using such facilities will speed your response, which might be an advantage, and will show something of your enterprise and computer skills. However, the responses to job advertisements may be sifted first by someone with little technical skill or interest, and an application sent online will lack the good presentation you can achieve with the printed page. There is also the danger of too swift a response: the job you get or fail to get may influence the whole of your working life, and it is worth taking time and care rather than going automatically for the most rapid form of reply.

There's another possible hazard. If the company you are applying to uses an agency to sift the applications, the agency itself may e-mail the chosen applications through to the personnel department, thus potentially losing something of your carefully prepared layout. Take the copy of your form/CV and letter with you to the interview, so that you can produce it if appropriate – I've heard of a case in which a section of the CV, lost in the transmission, was supplied by the candidate at the interview stage.

When you have posted your application form or CV, with its covering letter, you will have a long and frustrating wait to hear whether you are being called for interview. Use this time: watch the papers for any significant news about 'your' company, or about that sector of industry; talk to other people doing similar work; check the company's website for any developments. This will help you to feel that you are still advancing your career, and it may be of great value if you are called for an interview.

There is one other use of this time: look for other jobs. Even though the post you have applied for seems to be exactly what you want, you may not get it. You may not even get an interview. This is very disappointing, but you will be helped by having one or two other applications in mind. Next time, you may be successful.

▶ Example CV and covering letter

As an example of all this good advice about CVs and covering letters, I've invented a physics graduate who is applying for a job as a development engineer. You will see how she has emphasised her academic achievements and work experience in her CV; in her short covering letter, she has highlighted the factors which might make her stand out from other applicants, together with an indication of why she is attracted to the company. If you take this as your guideline, make sure that you think through and emphasise your achievements in a similar way. Be honest but don't undersell your good qualities; you want the job, so make sure that your readers recognise that fact too.

Curriculum Vitae

Jennifer Ann Hastings

Date of birth   14 May 1977

Nationality   British

Home address   23 Station Road, Westford, Somerset WF16 9HD

Telephone   0199 97777

EDUCATION

1996–2000   **University of Abimouth,**
                    including one year at the University of Poitiers,
                    France

                    Degree: MPhys, 2.1

Course at Abimouth

My fourth year included compulsory units in Quantum Theory, Electromagnetic Waves, Nuclear and Particle Physics and Advanced Experimental Physics. I also followed a course in Project Planning, which I found particularly interesting and helpful.

My final report topic was *Structure and Electrical Conduction in an Organic Polymer*; I was able to include information obtained during my vacation work with A B Ross Limited.

In my first and second years at University, I followed the language options, completing a course in French which prepared me for the year abroad.

Course at Poitiers

My third year was spent studying physics at the University of Poitiers. During this time, I took courses from the *Licence* year; these were closely linked to my final year study at Abimouth. I became proficient in French scientific language and was able to lead a seminar group in French.

1990–1996   **Westford Comprehensive School**
3 A Levels – Physics (A), French (A) and Mathematics (B)
10 GCSEs – including English Language,
Mathematics and French.

WORK EXPERIENCE

Summer 1998 **Technical Assistant, A B Ross Limited**
Working on a project concerned with reducing energy loss in overhead cables, I gained knowledge and experience which were subsequently used in my final year project at University.

During the three months of this work, I was part of a project team; the experience of working as part of a group has been useful to me in my final year. I also improved my communication skills, especially by taking part in a Presentations course organised by the company.

Summer 1997 Assistant, WHSmith, Westford

I gained experience in meeting the public in a working capacity, and was trained in the use of the till and the computer stock control system.

ADDITIONAL QUALIFICATIONS

I speak French fluently, and have conversational Spanish and a reading knowledge of German. I hope to be able to use these languages in my work.

I have attended courses organised by the University's Computer Services Centre on word processing, spreadsheets and compiling databases. I have used Word and Excel, and PowerPoint for my presentations.

I have held a clean driving licence since 1996.

INTERESTS

Through the University Physics Society, I became a Student Member of the Institute of Physics, and I have enjoyed taking part in meetings. During the Easter vacation in my second year, I took part in a weekend visit, organised by the Society, to CERN in Geneva.

Throughout my time at University, I have been an active member of the University Singers, taking part regularly in concerts at the University and in the area; in my final year, I was Treasurer, and had responsibility for the financial arrangements on these occasions. Music is a major interest, and I have continued to have lessons on the violin, reaching Grade 5 earlier this year.

Tennis and walking are my main outdoor activities, and I am a member of the University Sports Centre.

The names and addresses of two referees are available on request.

Covering letter

23 Station Road
Westford
Somerset
WF16 9HD

14 July 2000

Jane Goddard
Personnel Manager
Scott Baddeley Perkins Ltd
107 City Road
London WC3 9RJ

Dear Ms Goddard

Your ref: 1990/DE

I wish to apply for the post of Development Engineer, advertised recently within the Careers Service at Abimouth University. My CV is enclosed.

This position attracts me very much, partly because of the extensive graduate industrial training programme you offer, and partly because of your international scope; I should hope in the future to have the opportunity to work overseas with your company.

I feel that I have the appropriate key skills and experience, including:

- a thorough knowledge of my subject, as shown in my degree result; my final report, using information from my industrial experience, received a first class mark
- a high degree of computer literacy, including experience in compiling databases
- the ability to speak and write French fluently, combined with experience of living and working abroad; I also have useful knowledge of Spanish and German
- excellent communication skills: I have made presentations in-company and at the University in both English and French

- enjoyment of being part of a team; I worked as a member of a project team at A B Ross Limited for three months, and found that I could relate well to colleagues and enjoy a lively exchange of ideas.

As you will see from my CV, I have a particular interest in problems of energy loss. If I am successful in this application, I should welcome the chance to use my knowledge and experience in further investigation of this area of work.

I am available for interview at any time and, if appointed, would be able to start work within two weeks.

I look forward to hearing from you.

Yours sincerely

[signature]

Jennifer Hastings

▶ Key points

▶ Ask advice about possible careers as early as possible; your Careers Advisory Service will be able to assess where your strengths and weaknesses lie

▶ Take time over completing application forms; check the information in the advert, try out a photocopy first (or a spare copy if you have downloaded it), and note the date by which it has to be received. Speak to referees as soon as you can

▶ Always tell the truth in applying for work, at the same time stressing your good points

▶ Use any work experience you have had, however unlikely or irrelevant it may appear to be. Your leisure activities may also provide additional and useful experience

▶ Decide why you would like, and would be good at, this particular job, and make sure that the message comes through

▶ If you prepare a CV, plan its layout carefully, following modern conventions

► Always work backwards from the most recent experience, which is likely to be of most interest to the reader
► Send a covering letter with all applications. It gives you an extra opportunity to sell yourself, but keep it brief. Match what you say to the requirements given in the company's information
► Follow the conventions of letter writing, and check everything

10 The Successful Job Interview

A little while ago, you completed a carefully prepared, well-presented application form or CV, and sent it off. You have waited anxiously for a response, and at last it has arrived: you have been asked to attend an interview. Your reaction will probably be in two stages – first, pleasure that your application has been so well received, and second, nervous tension, in case you don't live up to it in a personal interview.

Both reactions are appropriate. Employers don't want to waste their own time by interviewing unsuitable candidates, and so the very fact that you have been selected for an interview means that your prospective employer was attracted by the information you presented: your qualifications seemed appropriate, and you yourself sounded as if you might make a useful colleague. So far, so good. However, you are right to be nervous; there is always an element of the unknown about an interview, and the strength of the 'opposition' is likely to be part of that unknown quantity, as is the exact nature of the interview when it happens.

Interviews take many forms, and may include a variety of tests and exercises; you can get help with these from your Careers Advisory Service, and if you haven't already done so, make an appointment to get some practice as soon as you can. This chapter concentrates on the communication aspects of the interview, principally preparing yourself beforehand, and then answering questions in a professional way; you may also have to make a presentation as part of your interview, as this is increasingly part of companies' selection procedures, and this is discussed briefly – the earlier chapters on giving a presentation are invaluable at this point.

Look carefully at the letter you have received from the company, and find out as much as you can about the form of the interview. If you are expected to stay overnight, you will be given information about accommodation; if the interview is to be on company premises, there is likely to be a map. You may be given a programme for the day, or asked to bring a short presentation with you. Make a careful note of the details you have been given, and think about what they reveal. It's very important that you don't miss part of the necessary preparation, or make a mistake about the date, time, or place. However, some first interviews are held on university or college premises, perhaps as part of a 'milk round', and it's worth looking briefly at these before considering the main interview or interviews, which are likely to be held on company premises.

▶ 'Milk round' interviews

The so-called 'milk round' is less popular than it used to be; you may not even be aware of it, still less take part. Nevertheless, some companies still like to visit educational establishments to meet prospective graduates and to make some preliminary moves towards attracting likely young people.

This stage is very much a two-way process. You are being given the chance to meet someone from a company you might want to work for, to ask questions and to assess how far you are genuinely interested in the prospects on offer. You may already have sent an application form, or you may be asked to complete one after your interview. From the company's point of view as well as from your own, this is an introductory stage in the process.

No company wants to visit every institution of further or higher education, and so there will already have been a preliminary selection procedure; most companies look at organisations which have appropriate courses, and of which they have had good experience in the past. So if you go to an interview of this sort, you can be reasonably sure that your course has given you the right background knowledge and appropriate experience for the job. The company is also aware of this, and so at this stage the interviewers are more likely to be interested in different information, such as whether you show real interest in and enthusiasm for your work so far, whether you would make a friendly, co-operative colleague, and whether you have business, as well as scientific or technical, abilities.

As a result, the person interviewing you is likely to be part of a human resources team rather than a scientific or technical expert. If you find that this is so, try not to use technical jargon in your answers, and make sure that you don't sound patronising to someone who may know less about your subject than you do. You need to get a feel for the company, and for possible opportunities; he or she wants to know about you, not least how well you relate to non-specialists. You are likely to be asked about your course in terms of what you enjoyed or liked least, and about your special project, not in terms of technical knowledge, but in terms of your attitude. Did you enjoy being part of a team, and if so, why? How did you decide about a sensible division of labour between you? What aspects of the project were the most interesting? One industrial interviewer says that he always asks 'How is your project going to affect my life?', not because he sees student projects as world-shaking pieces of research, but to see how the interviewees answer. If the commercial or social aspects of the topic have been considered, even if realistically there aren't any, all is well; if interviewees look bemused and say nothing, this will count against them – after all, each company is a business concern, and will want to ensure that its employees have some sense of commercial values.

You may also be asked about your outside interests, your long-term ambitions (have some prepared, but don't commit yourself too strongly to what you want to be doing in ten years' time – flexibility is important!), and your ability to communicate. These are all questions which you can foresee and prepare for. In the days before your interview, think through your course, noting the parts you particularly liked or are conscious of having done well in; think about the aspects of your course which you didn't enjoy, and try to analyse why – if your reasons might also apply to the work which you are applying for, you might want to think again. Remind yourself of your special interest areas or projects, and see if you can link them to the work you might be doing. Look again at the copy of your application, and decide what you might be asked about; don't undervalue your experience – you have almost certainly had to work as part of a team, to be involved in decision-making, to present your topic to your peers; all these have given you experience which will be useful to you in whatever capacity you are to be employed.

Your next stage of preparation is to check up on your knowledge of the industry and of the company itself. Talk to people who work in the same field, and to friends who have already had similar interviews. Read the business section of your daily paper, look at the company's website, listen to business programmes on the radio or television. Make sure that you keep up to date with the general news, too, as it may have a bearing on your area of work; it can also sound impressive if you make a comment which shows how up to date your knowledge is and how carefully you have thought about the implications of what you have read or heard.

This first part of the selection process will probably be informal, more like a friendly chat than a formal interview, but don't allow yourself to become too relaxed. Students often find an interview on their educational premises difficult to handle just because it doesn't feel like a formal occasion; they forget to dress appropriately, and tend to slouch rather than to walk and sit in a businesslike way. It's also too easy to ramble in giving an answer, and to say something casually which would be better left unsaid. Treat the occasion as a formal interview, and if it seems appropriate to relax a bit, do so outwardly but pay close attention to all that is said, by you or to you, throughout the conversation. Make eye contact with your interviewer, and at the end, smile and thank him or her for their time; this is a courtesy and also practical sense – you don't know when or how you may meet again, or how influential this person may be in your future.

There is an overlap between the milk round interview and the first interview proper; because of this, I will deal more fully with appropriate body language in discussing later interviews (see page 187). A modern development which may intervene is the telephone interview, which is tending to replace the milk round, and which may become even more important in the future.

▶ The telephone interview

A terrible scenario was presented by Peter Kingston in *The Guardian* (*Guardian Higher*, Tuesday 2 March, 1999). It was ten o'clock in the morning, and nobody was awake in the student house when the phone rang. A friend of the prospective employee answered in a befuddled way, and then shouted that 'a posh sounding geezer wants you on the phone'. The hopeful employee eventually managed to get downstairs, and immediately asked what time it was. He was told the time, and also that this was the beginning of a telephone interview for the job he'd applied for. His response to this news came in language which might be deemed inappropriate when used to a future employer. Except that by that time, the interviewer had probably become a might-have-been employer.

It's not only a dreadful scenario, it's a horribly realistic one. Employers are increasingly conducting preliminary interviews by telephone, and although in most cases the time of the call is pre-arranged, this cannot be guaranteed; everyone sharing the student's accommodation needs to be warned that when applications have been sent, the telephone must be answered at least politely and a message taken if necessary.

In spite of this dire warning, there are some advantages in this type of interview as long as the interviewee has advance warning. It is unlikely to be long – about 10 to 15 minutes seems the norm – and you can have notes prepared and available in a way which would be impossible if you could be seen. Plan what you want to ask; think of the main points of your experience and interests which you want to emphasise, and write these down in note form. While you are being interviewed, you can move reasonably freely from note to note, or add comments to your notes if it would be useful to do so.

Having prepared your notes, think about your self-preparation. Obviously, you don't have to wear a suit for a telephone interview, but you do need to think about your instinctive reactions. If you talk on the phone to a close friend, you may lean back, speak casually and even hold a different conversation with someone in the room, more or less at the same time. If you are to be interviewed, you need to have the room to yourself, if possible warning other people that you don't want interruptions. You will speak more formally if you sit in an upright, businesslike way, looking (and feeling) alert. Be ready a few minutes before the agreed time, and make sure that all your notes are within reach. Check the name of the interviewer, and make sure that your greeting is friendly and confident. Tone of voice is very important at any time, but especially so in the absence of visual contact; listen carefully to what is said and the way in which it is said, and make sure that your own response is bright and clear. Don't be tempted to talk for too long: when you have answered the question adequately, stop and wait for a follow-up. Don't interrupt, even if you are sure what the question is going to be; let the interviewer finish before responding.

Silence can present a problem in a telephone conversation, and so if you need to think for a moment before answering a question, let the interviewer know. There is no disgrace in asking for a minute to think through what you want to say, and it's far better than answering off the cuff and regretting it later. You will have planned one or two questions of your own; use them if you are given the opportunity, but keep them short – the call is taking time and costing money from the interviewer's point of view. As in any interview, thank the interviewer at the end, with a smile. The person at the other end of the line can't see the smile, but can hear it in your voice. Practise a telephone interview beforehand with a friend, and notice how the voice is brightened by a smiling friendly face.

▶ The first interview

This section discusses the first interview at which you are called to go to your prospective employer's place of work. It may be the sole interview, in which case it will take on some of the characteristics which will be discussed later in the section on second interviews, but it's quite possible that you will have two separate sessions, especially if you have applied to a large organisation. If this happens, it's likely that the first will be by human resources staff and the second by scientific or technical people, possibly including the manager with whom you will be working if you are appointed.

Even before you knew that you had an interview, you were preparing for the possibility by looking out for information about 'your' industry and 'your' company. When you know that you will soon have an interview, this activity becomes even more important. You will now need to check with the careers service, in case they have any useful up-to-date information – they will also, of course, help you with your general preparation for interview, and may even give you a trial run.

You will be glad that you kept a copy of your application form, as it reminds you of exactly what you said. Go through it, making notes of the details which are likely to produce questions, especially of the 'why do you want to work in this industry/for us' type. Clarify your answers to these questions, as they are very likely to be asked again, and now probably followed up in more detail. Think of examples from your own experience of occasions when you were part of a team, had to take a leadership role, had to explain a difficult concept to a non-specialist – all of these will be useful to you in answering questions. It's possible that your department or faculty will keep a book of questions asked at interview, for the benefit of future students; if so, work through it carefully, preferably with a couple of friends so that you can discuss how you would handle any difficulties.

There are practical considerations about arriving at the interview itself. How long will it take you to get there? Is it sensible to travel the previous day (if necessary, ring the company and ask about accommodation). If you can, go through the journey in advance, especially if you are going to drive, and find out exactly how long it's likely to take – remembering that if you will have to travel in the rush hour, you must allow longer. It's very important that you arrive in plenty of time, that is, that you reach your destination about 15 minutes before the appointment; obviously, you will want to get to the town or city with considerably more time in hand – generally speaking, the longer the distance, the more time you must allow for holdups on the way.

You must also decide on appropriate dress. This will depend to a certain extent on your area of work, but the chances are that you will need to look smart and formal – a suit and quietly coloured blouse/shirt is almost always acceptable. If you have any doubts about suitable dress, ask the advice of friends who have already been through interviews, or your tutor. Avoid anything which looks showy, such as distracting jewellery or brightly coloured socks. Check all the details – dirty shoes still act as a deterrent to prospective employers! It isn't a good idea to wear something which is completely new: it can prove to be uncomfortable, or to ride up in an embarrassing way, or to have some defect which becomes apparent at the wrong moment. Try your outfit on a few days before the interview, so that you know it will not distract you, or the interviewer, in any way.

You will be very pleased that you've been through all this preparation when you arrive for your interview, not least because you will feel confident that you can do your best. You will naturally feel nervous, but as with a presentation (see page 133), this is a good thing; it would be a serious disadvantage to be overconfident or casual, especially if your interviewers were aware of this – as is likely, given their training and experience. They won't worry in the slightest if you appear to be nervous, as long as you don't let the nerves overwhelm you.

When you reach your destination, explain to the person on the reception desk that you have come for interview, and give the interviewer's name and the time at which you are expected. If you have to sit and wait, look at a company brochure or magazine; it may give you a useful piece of information. You may find that other candidates are waiting at the same time; greet them in a friendly way, but don't start asking questions. If you do, they may sound better qualified than you, and this would undermine your confidence; don't try to put them down in any way, not least since you might have to work with them in the future!

As you wait, try some breathing exercises, as you did before you made a presentation. Take a deep breath, hold it and then let it out slowly, in a controlled way. Check that your shoulders aren't hunched up by the tension, and then breathe in the same way again. This will help you to relax, and to feel more confident.

When you are asked to go in for your interview, walk briskly with your head up, smile at the interviewers (there may be just one, but it's more likely that you will have a panel), and wait. One of them will probably greet you (respond with a smile), introduce himself or herself, and offer to shake hands. Do so firmly; a limp handshake can be off-putting. Follow the pattern indicated: you may need to shake hands with each member of the panel or just with the person chairing the session; sit down only when invited (sit back in your chair so that you appear upright and alert; don't fidget). Almost certainly the first one or two questions will be intended to help you relax, and so they will be easy to answer – 'Did you find us easily?', 'Did you have a good journey?', 'Have you been to this city/area before?' Give your answers clearly and briefly; they certainly don't want a blow by blow account of the problems you had finding the right bus.

All this is preamble, but an important part of the interview. There is courtesy on the part of the interviewers; indeed, if they didn't introduce themselves and give you a chance to settle down, you would start to have reservations about them – after all, you want to know whether they would make good colleagues for you, as well as the other way round. In these first few minutes, a great deal of communication is taking place, although only a small part of it is in words. They are assessing you: do you appear confident (but not too much so); do you respond swiftly and easily to them; is your general appearance appropriate; do you make eye contact immediately when someone speaks to you? Don't underestimate the impact of these things; what they may really be checking is how you would appear to one of their customers. Would your manner create an immediate good impression, even if you were under pressure at the time, as you are at present?

After the first few minutes, the questions will be more incisive, and perhaps challenging. Think ahead as far as you can: an apparently simple question may be followed up by a more searching one. 'Are you good at communicating with non-specialists?' 'Yes' (of course). 'So, tell me about some of the difficulties you met when you were working on your final project.' (You need to have thought about this, and perhaps chosen one problem which was managerial rather than scientific, and another which was, for example, to do with choosing a piece of equipment which was all you could afford although you knew that the best was too expensive – don't rush straight into a complex scientific or technical problem which demands professional knowledge just because you think it will impress; the effect will be just the opposite.)

Some questions have a built-in trap which you might not see until it's too late. 'Do you see yourself primarily as a good team player or as a leader?' is typical of this type: say that you're a good team player and you might be saying that you lack leadership qualities; say that you're a natural leader, and you sound arrogant. Refuse to pigeonhole yourself. Say that it depends on circumstances, that you've always enjoyed being part of a team but you did take particular responsibility for ... and you feel that when you've had more work experience, you'd enjoy the challenge. Let them see that you want to keep your options open, and that you can recognise a catch question when you see one.

As you answer, make eye contact mainly with the questioner, but don't forget the other people present; they need to be included from time to time. Don't go on too long: two problems are enough, and there may be yet another follow-up question: 'So how did you set about getting everyone to agree over the equipment, given the strength of feeling?' 'How did you help those who still disagreed to feel part of the team, so they weren't tempted to opt out?' These are very important questions; you may be appointed as a junior member of the team, but your interviewers want to know whether you have the makings of a good project manager in the future.

If you don't understand a question, ask for it to be repeated. If you don't know the answer, say so. There is no disgrace in asking for clarification, or being honest enough to admit ignorance, but trying to bluff or to pretend to know when you don't is always dangerous – if you respond like this, you may be seen as the sort of person who in the future would take chances which involve the safety of other people or large amounts of company money.

On the whole, it's better to give a short answer, as long as it isn't clearly inadequate, than to talk too much. The questioner can always ask for more information, or you could offer it: 'As you can see, I'm very enthusiastic about this, and I can go into more detail if you'd like me to.' This allows the interviewer to take the initiative, but gives you the chance to show that you are confident in your own knowledge.

You will probably be asked about your hopes for the future, your leisure activities (think in advance how they relate to work experience – teamwork, taking risks, deep concentration, ability to work independently), any language ability or other skill you've mentioned on your application form; perhaps (a tricky question) how you would expect the company to develop your skills in the future.

You will also be asked if there is anything you'd like to ask them. Prepare two or three questions: further training is always a good subject to discuss, or opportunities to find out about different areas of the company's work or to use a particular skill. Never ask about money! If you find that all your questions have already been answered, say so, and thank your interviewers.

You are still being interviewed until the door has closed behind you. Don't look relieved that it's over, heave a sigh, slump in your chair or rush out of the room. You might be stopped at the last minute with an extra question, and you are certainly being watched. Having thanked your interviewers with a smile, you walk steadily and confidently out, close the door behind you and then relax.

▶ The second interview

It would be lovely, in that first feeling of relief that your interview is over, to think that you would now be offered a job. This may happen, but quite possibly the whole ordeal will be repeated in a further, and usually more testing, interview at the employer's premises. At least you have the comfort of knowing that you passed the first test, and that the company is sufficiently impressed to want to see you again.

Assuming that you still want the job, you need to prepare in the same way for the second interview: find out all you can about your prospective employer, read good newspapers and check the Internet, and discuss interview techniques with colleagues and your careers advisers. There is more: this second interview will almost certainly be scientifically or technically challenging, and you need to ensure that your professional knowledge is up to date and firmly in your mind.

This time, you will be facing people who have expertise in your area of study; they may include your future line manager or project leader. The company liked the sound of you as a person in your first interview, and now they want to make sure that you are among the brightest and most enthusiastic of all the young people available. Go back yet again to your course, analyse especially any choices you had to make about special subjects; think of the technical implications of your final year's work and especially your project or dissertation. Consider any further work in this field that might be feasible, and how your work could relate to that carried out by the company.

This is likely to be a longer interview and you may be required to prepare material in advance, especially a presentation. You have probably made presentations as part of your course, and so it's a good idea to look at any handouts you were given, and to reread Chapters 6 and 7 of this book.

You may, although at this stage it's unlikely, be given a topic to research and present. This has the advantage of giving you a starting point; you will almost certainly have to narrow the topic down to be able to deal adequately with your material in the time allotted (probably about 10 minutes). Don't panic if the subject is one about which you don't know much. Others will be in the same position, and you know from experience how little you can actually say in such a limited time. Research your limited area as thoroughly as time permits, and ask advice from your tutor or an appropriate lecturer.

It's much more likely, however, that you will either be told to prepare a short presentation about some scientific or technical topic that interests you, or that you will be given a totally free hand – 'present on any subject you like'. Let's look at the former situation first.

What are the possibilities? You could use part of your final project. If you do this, your interviewers will know what you have done (which isn't to say that it's a bad thing to do); you may have too much material, and it may originally have been shared with somebody else. The other problem is that your interviewers will be familiar with such topics and may be bored by them. You could do a 'follow-up' to your project, selecting one idea which needed further work, and developing this yourself, with your supervisor's help. This has obvious advantages, but it entails extra work – do you have the time and the facilities? You may look outside your course, and talk about something which you were involved with on a vacation job. This could have advantages. You will be looking afresh at a topic rather than going back to one which you may feel has haunted you for months; it will have an industrial or commercial setting, and it is likely to be different from other people's presentations. Obviously, you must ensure that you don't reveal anything which is commercially sensitive – contact the person you worked with and ask permission. You may have an outside interest which is technical or scientific in nature, and so choose to talk about that, with the advantage that you are naturally enthusiastic or you wouldn't be involved with the subject, and again, it will be different from a 'standard' educational project.

These are only possibilities, and you must think carefully about your choice. Try not to involve yourself in too much extra work (remember that you have to answer questions on the topic you choose), but if you can, avoid a subject which you have been involved with for so long that you're tired of it. Remember that your choice of topic is probably not of great importance; what you make of it is likely to matter more.

If you are given a completely free choice, you have in some ways a much bigger problem. Your first decision is whether to be scientific at all. Your second is to find a topic which is small enough to be handled reasonably in a very short time. Your third is rather different – choosing something which will make you stand out. You may need to look carefully at your outside interests. Is there anything which is unusual? Have you travelled in a remote, perhaps dangerous, part of the world? (Remember that nowadays students often travel widely, and you don't want to give the third presentation of the day on adventures in Thailand.) In talking about this subject with newly employed gradu- ates, I heard that a memorable presentation had been given on the technicalities of bell-ringing (it had been followed quickly by the offer of a job). However, you can't at this stage develop an exotic hobby in time for the interview, and so you may need to look again at work experience, or, if absolutely necessary, at your course. Your choice shouldn't be trivial, but it should be something in which you are genuinely interested.

When you have chosen your topic, you need to prepare it in line with advice given earlier in this book. A useful comment was made by a regular interviewer in a large engineering company. He pointed out that one of the prime characteristics of prospective employees which interested the company was self-organisation. Can you prioritise? How is your time management? Can you work well under time pressure? One very good way in which he felt that he could assess the answer to these important questions was through the presentation. Did the candi- date keep to the time given? Had the preparation itself been well organ- ised? A common problem, he said, was that people spent far too long producing elaborate and effective visual aids, and didn't think enough about the information. Have the answers to obvious questions been planned in advance? This shows an ability to think through a problem and to predict areas of concern – very useful attributes to any company.

The question of visual aids is a serious one. You want to show your knowledge of how they can be used effectively, but you are unsure about the equipment. This is where foresight is impressive: you ring and ask what will be available in the room on the day; the chances are that the answer will be the overhead projector, and you now know what type of visual material to prepare. Unless you are specifically asked to use a data projector, don't risk it. Too much can go wrong (see page 127), and you have enough to worry about during your interview without extra problems of compatibility or using a strange laptop or taking too long to boot the whole system up. Prepare good quality overhead acetates, using colour if it's appropriate, and then you don't need to worry any further.

Nevertheless, the importance of preparing and rehearsing the presentation thoroughly, with your visual aids, can hardly be exaggerated: it shows personal organisation, management skills, and your ability to communicate well under stress. For these precise reasons, presentations have become increasingly important at all levels of the selection process – a recent applicant for a chief executive's post was told as soon as she appeared at the formal interview that she had been the only one of half a dozen experienced interviewees to keep to time in her presentation. She got the job.

So you have a great deal of work to do in preparation for your second interview, which may start not with questions but with a dinner the night before. You may, of course, be told that this is not a part of the interview process, but you would do well to ignore such a comment – of course you will be assessed in an informal way during the evening. Nevertheless, try to behave as naturally as you can; be very polite and friendly to the other candidates; don't try to show off; don't drink too much; don't relax so much that you aren't thinking about what you're saying. You need to show how well you can relate to strangers – ask about their interests or the place they come from, rather than just talking about yourself.

Such 'social' occasions can be a great strain, as can 'free' time during the next day, but it's useful to remember that everyone will feel the same way. The programme is likely to include a range of activities such as psychometric tests, group work, case studies and timed exercises, which are outside the scope of this book but not of your careers advisers. Working in a group presents some difficulty, in that you want to make a mark, but not to be seen to dominate; being aware of this problem is at least halfway to solving it. If you feel that some stage of the programme has gone badly, don't allow yourself to lose confidence. It's unlikely that anyone has sailed through the whole day without some difficulty or self-doubt, and your worry may have been much less obvious to others than it was to you. Above all, don't give up. Even if you don't get this job, look on it as good experience for next time.

So at last you get to the interview itself, probably with a panel of three people. The advice about non-verbal behaviour which I gave earlier (see page 187) still applies; believe that you've done well so far, and feel and look as confident as you can. This interview may well be very demanding, with difficult technical questions and frequent 'what would you do if' scenarios. As before, if you don't know the answer, say so, but as far as you can, give thoughtful, reasoned responses. If you need time to think, ask for it. Don't show anxiety if you realise that you've given a poor answer. If you can think of a way to improve it, say

'I think I could express that better as ... ' or 'May I add to that answer ... ', but if you can't, let it go and continue to look and sound professional. Make eye contact as you answer – you may feel a bit as if you're under attack on all fronts, but the other candidates will have to face the same problems.

You won't be expected to know everything, and maintaining a professional relationship with the panel is of critical importance: don't let your answers ramble on, never become aggressive, even if you feel that a question is unfair (it might have been asked purely to see how you reacted), listen carefully to the questions and answer the one you are asked rather than the one you wish you had been asked. Remember that I suggested breathing exercises while you waited for your interview to start (see page 187). If there is a pause during the interview when the attention is off you (this often happens as one interviewer hands over to another for the next question), take as good a breath as you can without it being obvious, relax your shoulders, and let the breath out slowly. Nobody is likely to notice, but you will feel more in control as a result.

As before, keep up the professionalism until the day is completely over, and don't allow yourself to be too discouraged, even if you feel that it didn't go well. You might have been much more impressive than you thought you were, and in any case, it was very good experience. If you don't get the job, you have nothing to lose by ringing the human resources person you met earlier and asking where the weaknesses were. You might get some good advice and a pointer for the future, and the person you speak to will be impressed by your thoroughness.

This book has looked at communication in a wide variety of the situations you may meet during your career as a student. This is perhaps the most important aspect of your course. If you lack scientific or technical knowledge, that can be put right when it becomes necessary – you are in any case likely to have further training when you are at work. If you communicate well, during your course and at work, you have an invaluable tool in sharing your knowledge with friends, colleagues, and, eventually, customers and clients; this may indeed be the basis of your success. Good luck!

► **Key points**

► Before you go to an interview, find out about the organisation you
  have applied to. Check for up-to-date information in newspapers
  and on the company's website
► At a first interview, you are likely to be asked about your attitudes,
  your interest in your work and its commercial implications, and
  similar questions designed to check whether they want you as a
  colleague
► Be prepared for a preliminary interview by telephone. Make sure
  that the tone of your voice is friendly and confident
► Before an on-site interview, check details of travel and accommodation. Arrive in plenty of time, and be well prepared
► Remember the importance of first impressions, yours as well as
  theirs. How would you appear to a customer; do they seem to you
  to be desirable colleagues?
► If you have to give a presentation, prepare it carefully; think about
  likely questions
► During your interview, give thoughtful, reasoned responses, don't
  rush your answers, and say if you don't know
► Don't relax until you are out of the room

Further Reading

Kirkman, John: *Good Style: Writing for Science and Technology*, Spon, 1992

Lindsay, David: *A Guide to Scientific Writing*, Longman, 2nd edn 1995

Peck, John and Coyle, Martin: *The Student's Guide to Writing*, Macmillan, 1999

van Emden, Joan: *A Handbook of Writing for Engineers*, Macmillan, 2nd edn 1998

van Emden, Joan and Easteal, Jennifer: *Technical Writing and Speaking: An Introduction*, McGraw-Hill, 1996

Index